Miss Conception is a must read for those who have fears that hold them back, who feel the need to be perfect or who think others have a perfect life and view their own lives as less than perfect. Lisa's raw transparency will help you to embrace your imperfectness and achieve what you want in life.

Jill Kopanis
National Speaker-Shazam Communications

I recommend women of ALL ages take advantage of reading *Miss Conception*. It is a transparent story that I believe every woman can relate to. The lessons taught bring to light the fact that most women are caught in the trap between what our society and the media says we should look like and have and the reality of everyday truth. As author of *RISE…What To Do When Hell Won't Back Off*, I know how easy it is to hide behind a personally designed mask. Lisa exposes her personal misconceptions and masks as she teaches woman worldwide that you do not have to be a beauty queen to have a "Crowning Moment".

Debra Hayes
Author/Speaker/Coach—www.Debralynnhayes.com

ENDORSEMENTS

MISS CONCEPTION

Our world is a world of images. Technology, the Internet, Pinterest, Facebook, Twitter—all of them profess the power of image. How much easier it is to watch a short video than read an instruction booklet. Ideas are implanted in our brain via images. The marketing machine propaganda has become so powerful it tells you how to think, how to act, what's important, what's right and wrong, and what *you need* to be happy. We are taught and told through these images that if we do not have a certain look, forget it. We cannot succeed in business, in relationships, in life. We see pictures of actors and actresses who have the right shape, the right legs, the awesome butt, the powerful chest—and spend our lives striving to achieve that same image. We have become convinced that happiness, *true* happiness, is right around the corner if we can just get… or do…or meet… all based on images we see.

Body image is no exception. From a very young age the female child sees the perfect proportions of her favorite Disney princess. The Princess's happiness, acceptances and love—even from her family—revolve around her beauty. It goes without saying that the beautiful character gets the boy, the castle, and happiness ever after. Woe to the child whose character and self-worth are built on that misconception. Our hearts should ache for the girls who really believe they don't have a chance at any of these without having that image.

Men and boys have similar concerns. If they do not have the image of the superhero with bulging biceps, a solid square jaw, thick flowing hair, and lightning reflexes and talent, they can forget about ever being accepted in society. They should make no attempt at success, but rather find relief and short-lived pleasure in seeking more artificial images on the Internet that further skew their perceptions of women and life.

We are in a crisis of character. Our self-worth, self-esteem, and actual ability to feel the joy of living are all based on false pretenses and artificial images. We are continually seeking happiness through acceptance from the world, rather than having joy in why we were created and in our creator.

I have been in the health and fitness field for over thirty-five years now. I have seen trends and fads come and go like the wind. New eating styles, new exercise programs, new drugs and supplements—everyone is looking for the next great thing in weight loss, body transformation, wealth, and health. All of them work for some; none of them work for all. Very rarely do any of them broach the real problems in life/health, the mental, spiritual, and emotional aspects. Few of us recognize that self-acceptance, relationships, and realization that image and body appearance, though at the forefront of most programs out there, are really the least important. We all age. We all change. No one remains 18 forever, even though that appears to be the goal and effort in everything professed as proper and correct in the world of health and fitness. Striving for that body image causes nothing but damage in the long run, yet we have all failed to see it. This struggle is not only a total lie but treacherous. Unnecessary surgeries, drugs, eating disorders—the list is extensive and dangerous. It is becoming so common place that we need solid, strong men and women to stand up and fight for what is right.

Lisa Moser is a woman who has stepped out, exposed herself with her story, and let it be known that the winner really is Misconception…unless you stop listening to the lies, trust in God, let the fear subside, know it is never too late, and that balance and joy in life provide fulfillment.

I have had the honor and privilege of knowing Lisa on a professional and personal level for some time now. She is a woman with a mission. Helping others obtain physical, mental, emotional, and spiritual health is her goal in life. She has surpassed even her own goals with her manuscript "**Miss Conception**", as there could not be a timelier book.

In her honest and personal story, Lisa allows the reader to step back and assess his or her own situation. Lisa's story provides honest and simple answers based on her experiences written in a way we can all relate to. She has done a wonderful job expressing this and making it obvious to anyone reading it that there is a solution that works.

I so enjoyed the book, it took me just a few hours to read it. I then walked right into my teenage daughter's room and handed her the book! This book is great for all ages, as it is plainly written and told in a way to keep you involved by allowing your own story to come out.

I could not be more excited about endorsing and sharing a book with my friends, colleagues, family and patients. It is so timely for the situation in our world, and it is something that could make a difference. Nice work, Lisa! I am already looking forward to reading your next one.

Dr. Warren Willey DO
Founding Diplomat: American Board of Holistic Medicine
Diplomat: American Board of Obesity Medicine
Diplomat: American Board of Family Medicine
Author of *What Does Your Doctor Look Like Naked?, Better Than Steroids, The Z Diet,* and *The T Club*
http://drwilley.com

When *Lisa Moser* reached out to me on Facebook saying she has been a fan of mine for years, I quickly discovered it's me who is ***her*** biggest fan! I'm drawn to her risk taking and her extraordinary tenacity to educate the world about diabetes. Her honesty and authenticity resonates whether she is speaking, reading from her children's book *I Know Someone with Diabetes* or the words she has delicately and beautifully placed together in her new release **Miss Conception**. I encourage you to join me in this *fan*-affair, this beauty is bound to inspire you!

Kathy Kaehler
Celebrity Trainer, Author & Better Living Expert

Miss Conception is exactly what you should read if you truly want to go after the life you want. The obstacles we face along the way—especially those we encounter internally—are ones we can tackle with the right mindset, attitude and confidence. Lisa Moser's experience and real world advice will help you achieve the goals you're after while respecting and overcoming the difficulties along the way. Don't let them hold you back. Read this book.

Amy Schmittauer
Best Selling Author of *Vlog Like a Boss,* Keynote Speaker and YouTuber

Miss Conception

5 Steps to Overcome our Misconceptions and Achieve our own Crowning Moments

Lisa Moser

Copyright © 2017 Lisa Moser
All rights reserved.

Printed in the United States of America

Published by Author Academy Elite
P.O. Box 43, Powell, OH 43035

All rights reserved. No part of this publication may be reproduced, stored in a retrieval system, or transmitted in any form or by any means—for example, electronic, photocopy, recording—without the prior written permission of the publisher. The only exception is brief quotations in printed reviews.

Paperback ISBN: 978-1-946114-38-9
Hardcover ISBN: 978-1-946114-39-6

Library of Congress Control Number: 2017901649

Cover design by MaryDes www.marydes.eu.
Interior design by JETLAUNCH.net
Crown artwork by Arlaina Moser

This book is dedicated to my husband Don, and my four amazing children Cambree, Arlaina, Noah, and Cohen. The very people that bring so much joy to my life.

Contents

Introduction: Let's Get Real!... 1

Miss Conception #1 3
Performance and Perfection = Love and Worth

    Your Crowning Moment 19
    It's Time To Move On

Miss Conception #2 27
If I Looked a Certain Way, I Would Be Happy.

    Your Crowning Moment 43
    Change your thoughts, Change your world.
    —Norman Vincent Peale

Miss Conception #3 55
FEAR—Stories We Tell Ourselves

    Your Crowning Moment 73
    If You Can't Beat Fear, Do it Scared.
    —Glennon Doyle Melton

Miss Conception #4 83
It's Too Late

Your Crowning Moment 95
Let's Dream Again

Miss Conception #5 107
Being Healthy Means Eating Salads

Your Crowning Moment 115
The More Balanced Your Life, The More Joy You Feel!

Foreword

Misconceptions. We all have dealt with them. Either through how others perceive us, or our own misconceptions of others. How we meet these attitudes and our reaction to the false beliefs can help shape the core foundation that molds us as adults. This is especially true in young women.

As an accomplished author, successful businesswoman and national pageant queen, Lisa Moser has had to deal head on with the misconceptions attached to pageantry and living life in the spotlight.

When I first met Lisa, I saw a confident person with an engaging smile and warmth that draws you in. As we became better acquainted, she shared about her battle with low self-esteem and body image issues throughout her life. It took intense work to become that confident woman.

She shared her aspiration to help women who face insecurities brought on by the media's ideals of what we should look like. As a result, Lisa has opened her heart and provided an honest look into how she has overcome the misconceptions of her life.

Lisa shares how to win your own crowns through debunking these common misconceptions:

- Performance and perfection equals love and worth
- Outward physical appearance can bring you happiness
- Being healthy means eating salads
- I can't do that, what will people think
- As we age, we lose the inspiration to create goals and dream

Through her stories and insights, Lisa shares her heart and provides a path to empowerment. She helps readers understand their self-worth while facing life head on. Best of all she demonstrates that you are never too old to chase your dreams.

Kary Oberbrunner
Author of *ELIXIR Project*, *Day Job to Dream Job*, *The Deeper Path*, and *Your Secret Name*

To my mother Sue, the first woman in my life that showed me what hard work and perseverance looked like.

To my sister Amy, for always having my back and being my biggest cheerleader.

Two amazing women in my life!

To all the amazing women that will read this book. May it resonate deep within your soul that you are beautiful and that life is meant to be an amazing journey!

I asked over 2000 people:

What is something people think about you that isn't necessarily true?

A "MISS CONCEPTION"

"I put on an air of being wealthy to fit in when in fact we have so much credit card debt it scares me."

"They think I am a pushover because I am nice to people."

"I am always the life of the party and the fun friend who always makes fun of herself to get laughs. I do this in hopes that people will like me because I really don't like myself very much. I want to change and be confident but I don't know where to start."

"I have always taken care of everyone. So the misconception is that I don't need someone to take care of me. I put up a strong front because I don't like to be vulnerable."

"They think I am wild because I have tattoos and purple hair."

"People think I am confident, but I am not."

"I am a total control freak. I need everything to look perfect so people think I have it all together. I don't."

"Sometimes because I always appear happy and positive, people think my life is easy or so called perfect. That is not true!"

"I do not like to show emotion (more specifically cry) in front of others to seem like I have it all together and can handle it."

"I never ask for help; I don't want others to think I am dependent on anyone."

"People think I am stuck up when in reality I am just very insecure."

"I act tough in front of others and say whatever I feel like, even if it hurts someone's feelings, not because I want to be mean but because I want to feel important. I honestly lack self-esteem.

"I live behind the misconception that I am less than all others; that I deserve the hardship and pain I experience because I am unworthy of true or real happiness."

"If I could find a great guy I would finally be happy."

"Everyone thinks because I am skinny that I don't eat anything. I actually eat all the time and I am so self-conscious of my body."

"At work I put on a mask of self-confidence and arrogance when in reality I am just wanting respect. I am really a nice person."

"People think because I am very well off financially that I have no worries—so far from the truth."

"They think I have it all together where in reality I have an alcohol problem."

"I live in fear of people discovering the real me."

"I feel sad every day when I leave my kids at daycare when I really want to be a stay-at-home mom. So I act like working is so important for women to protect my own feelings."

"I wish every day that I could have a career and not be a stay-at-home mom. I pretend that I think all moms should stay home with their kids because I don't want to be judged for wanting to go back to work."

"I push my kids to be exceptional so I look like a great parent."

"I have a teenager addicted to drugs and instead of sharing and letting people know our struggles, I hide the whole dark area of our lives as if it doesn't exist. I often wonder if I would get real, I could find other's that deal with the same issues."

To download workbook, go to
www.LisaMoser.com/workbook

Miss Conception

5 Steps to Overcome our Misconceptions and Achieve our own Crowning Moments

Don't compare your life to someone else's highlight reel. You never know where their journey has taken them.

Take your own journey.

Let's Get Real!

What a way to start a book, jumping in and being totally transparent! As I sit here to write, I am discovering that this is one of the most challenging things I have done to date and I have done a lot of challenging things in my life.

You see, God put it in my heart several years ago to write a book. I wasn't quite sure how I was going to do that or what it was going to be about, but I knew that was what I was being called to do. For the longest time I thought, *"How am I going to write a book; I'm not a writer, I'm a speaker,"* (and just in case you're wondering, I still thought that today as I am writing this!).

For a long time, I thought that I would just write about things that I have spoken about for years and help women discover their worth. What I didn't know was the direction that I would end up going: being totally introspective with you, letting you know *"things aren't always as they seem,"* and sharing my story so people can understand that life is so full of misconceptions that affects the way we live our lives.

So here I am, being very transparent and vulnerable in order to hopefully help free you from the feeling of inadequacy and pressure to be perfect. I feel as if more people would just get REAL with each other and stop the facade that we all have in some way, then we could learn to love and encourage each other and work to reach our potentials.

When I started thinking about where I should start, asking God what He might want me to share, I have to be honest, I wasn't crazy about the answer I was getting. Have any of you experienced that? When you ask God what to do but then don't like the answer? Not because I don't trust in His ways, but because it wasn't something that I already had prepared, nor was this going to be easy for me personally.

You see, what many of you probably don't know about me is that I am a speaker with a teaching heart. My job is to talk, and, as my husband and kids will tell you, I do it quite well! I have been doing public speaking for almost 25 years and have done hundreds of presentations—of all kinds.

I have spoken to groups ranging from 10 to 10,000 people. I have talks prepared for about everything from health and wellness and weight loss, to talks on change, second chances, and dreaming. The one topic I thought was perfect for a book was one that I use for a lot of the sports teams I speak to. It is about goal setting and our beliefs and desires to achieve something we set out as important to us. I thought that was a good topic for a book, one that I had tons of things already prepared. I thought it could be a great way to help people and move them towards their goals.

Anyway, what I wanted to write about, and what I felt led to share, were two different things. This is not going to be easy for me because it is a very personal story. It is a story about **misconceptions** and how the world saw me opposed to how I saw myself and what was really happening on the inside.

This is a story to help people see that things aren't always as they seem. I pray that sharing this story with you will help release something in you to be "real" and just find joy in your own life and stop comparing yourself to others.

MISS CONCEPTION #1

Performance and Perfection = Love and Worth

I grew up with the love of performing. From the time I can remember, if I wasn't lip syncing to my favorite Shaun Cassidy album, I was dancing in the living room. It gave me so much joy. I would do it day after day and know every word to every song on an album that I had and loved. When you're young, you have no concept of knowing if you are a good singer or a bad singer, you just know you love to sing. That's all that mattered then. I am sure you can relate in some way.

My favorite thing to do on the playground at school and at home was to play make-believe. I can remember in grade school there was a group of us that always played "Mod Squad" at recess. A 70s show about detectives that were solving crimes. I loved this show. The only female in the group of young detectives was a blond-haired, beautiful girl.

I had fabulous leadership skills when I was in grade school. I was always in charge of the group and told everyone what the script was for the day and who everyone's character was. My 4th grade teacher called it bossy, but when I see young girls like that today, I just see future leaders!

I had wonderful self-esteem back then, it just was a natural thing. In grade school, I never remember feelings of self-doubt or not being as good as someone else. I had no concept of our family not having much. What I do remember is it being cool that my mom was so young and pretty and people being confused as to why she had a different last name than me.

At recess when we played this make-believe detective game, I was always the beautiful make-believe girl. We would act out different scenes that we had strategically set for the day. My character would usually get kidnapped by a bad guy and they would search and do everything they could to get me back. It was acting at its finest! It was like my first non-paid acting job. I always just had so much fun and loved the drama of it all.

At home when I would play house with the neighbor kids, we would always pretend we had famous husbands and then decide how many kids we had. I was usually either married to Elvis Presley or Shaun Cassidy. If I wasn't lip-synching their songs in my bedroom, they were my husband in my make-believe world with my friends.

We would play outside for hours pretending we were a wonderful happy family. I still remember in the fall how we would outline the yard with all the fallen leaves and use them to mark where the walls of our house were and then put rooms in the house. It was one of my favorite things to do and a happy memory from my childhood.

During that time in grade-school, my mom signed me up to be on a youth football cheerleading squad. I loved being a cheerleader, and I loved doing the cheers and dance routines at the football games. I just loved acting and performing from a very young age.

I took that love into middle school and high school where I became a cheerleader. To me, there was something really exciting about leading a crowd at a sporting event and being in the limelight so to speak. I absolutely loved it! And with that love I found out that I enjoyed competition.

When I was in high school and became a varsity cheerleader, our coach was very much into competitive cheerleading, so we would practice all the time and go to competitions. We were really good. We worked really hard on dance numbers, cheers, and our incredible mounds. Back then you could build a human pyramid as high as you could go! We were known for our 4 high pyramid. We went to Chicago for several years and would win awards at national competitions. I loved competing, but I loved winning even more!

Another thing that I loved was that my mom and step-dad would come to the football games and watch me cheer. I relished in the feeling of them watching me and being proud of me. This is when the "performance-equals-worth-and-love" started to kick in. I just felt worthy when I was doing something that made my parents proud.

Performance and Perfection = Love and Worth

My parents divorced when I was 4 years old. They were very young and just were not meant to be together. Their story is not mine to tell, though I swear my mom should write a book about her life. She has endured a lot in her lifetime. All I can do is share how being from divorce affected my life. I think we all are affected by our childhood, good and bad, and it's just our decision how we choose to deal with the bad.

Coming from a divorce has its challenges to say the least, especially when your parents are young and still trying to figure out life themselves. All I can remember is feeling divided and pulled in two different directions. I think divorce does that to kids of all ages. When you're really young, you can't process the reasons for the divorce with any kind of rationality. All I really wanted was to be loved and feel loved. Anytime I could get attention from my parents, whatever kind of attention it was, I felt love. I think that is true for all kids when they are really young.

I remember I would try many different ways of getting that attention. One time I distinctly remember was at school. I remember pretending to twist my ankle on the playground and acting like it was hard to walk. At our elementary school, if you were hurt or sick they would let you lie on a cot in a small, closet-sized room until your parents would come get you.

I remember lying in there while they called my mom to come get me, wondering how I would sell her on the idea of my hurt ankle. I vividly remember hitting my ankle up against the brick wall so it would turn red and look like I really did hurt it. I guess in my little mind I just wanted their attention, because I thought attention meant love. I don't know why I thought that, but I did, and it stayed with me most of my life.

When I discovered cheerleading at that young age and had my mom and stepdad there to watch me, I felt that love.

It was how my youthful thinking processed it and continued to do so through high school.

During middle school and high school, I discovered that being a cheerleader and wearing a cute outfit got a lot of attention from the boys. There was even a time in high school when I worked in the office during one of the periods of the day. I would deliver notes or messages to the different classrooms to students.

During those times, everyone would be in their classrooms, so the hallways were pretty quiet. The only people in the halls were teachers or staff members that didn't have class. I can remember during the period of the day that I worked, when I would deliver these slips to the different classes, one of the male teachers that always had that class free would be in the hallway. He would always make comments to me about how great I looked in my skirt or my long legs or something to that extent—things that would get teachers fired today, but back then, it just was the way it was.

Similarly, during cheerleading practice, the male that helped us with gymnastics, would always make comments to me as well. I just took it as a compliment. This kind of thing happened a lot to me as a teenager, but I never saw it as something negative, I just saw it as attention, and attention meant worth in my mind. **(big misconception)**.

In my early 20's, a very dear woman, Val, introduced me to theater and the stage. She was my varsity cheerleading coach in high school, so she knew my love for performance. Val would direct these amazing theater productions in the summers. She reached out to me to come try out for her production of *Damn Yankees*.

I had never really been involved much in theater. I had done some shows in high school, but only in the dance course group. Never had I dreamed of trying out for a role back then. Honestly, I didn't know I had it in me; I always had really low self-esteem in high school (although if you asked anybody that knew me then they wouldn't say that. But I did). Val believed in me, she told me I could do it. She wanted me to try out for the lead role—what?!

If it wasn't for her believing in me and speaking into my life that I was a performer and I would be great at this, I probably would not have accomplished a lot of the things I did in my life. Sometimes it just takes that one person to believe in you the way you can't see. So I tried out and got the lead female role in a huge production. I was clueless as to what was to come but I was up for the challenge.

I discovered that I loved being on stage and performing and was quite good at it. I went on to have the lead roles in many theater productions. I was in *Seven Brides for Seven Brothers, Cinderella, Jesus Christ Superstar, They're Playing our Song, Christmas at the Palace*, just to name a few. I just loved the theater, performing, the family feel of the cast, and entertaining people and making them happy.

I also discovered that whenever I did a musical, especially when I had the lead role, I would get attention and feel worthy of something. This felt amazing to me, as I loved the feeling of working towards something and having people appreciate and love what I did.

However, more importantly, I thought they loved me because I did something special. My father would come and be front and center when

I did these things. I had finally found a way to make him proud of me and love me. Up until then, he had never really been to any of my cheerleading competitions, or the football games, and definitely not around for my lead role on the playground. But as the lead in a community musical that was getting press in the newspaper, radio, and on billboards across town, I had finally found something that made him proud (that was my misconception).

Miss Conception

From the time I was a little girl I remember sitting in front of the TV watching Miss USA or Miss America and dreaming of what it must be like to be on that stage competing. I remember thinking that those girls on that stage were from another planet or something. They were so perfect, so far from normal, so beyond anything that I can even comprehend.

I was so blown away by these women, and I loved watching them. At the end of the two hours of competition on television, somebody won a crown and was named "the most beautiful woman in the United States." I was always mesmerized by the sparkle and grandeur of the beauty pageants, and I watched them every year. Never did I dream that I would ever be one of those women, up on that stage on national television, because I was nothing like them at all.

When I was around 18 years old, a friend of mine talked me into competing at a little local pageant that was being held in our city. It was a preliminary to the Miss Ohio America pageant. I remember my first thought: "there is no way I could do this"! However, my love of performance and competition kicked in, so I said yes.

I had to have a talent, a bathing suit, and an evening gown. I asked Val to help me put together a singing and dancing routine for the talent, I used my prom dress for my gown, and got a bathing suit. I was ready to perform and compete. I didn't know at all what I was doing, but everyone telling me I was so tall and pretty and should be a model helped me think maybe I could do it.

Well, let's just say I didn't do so hot. I'll never forget sitting in that interview with these pageant judges and having no clue how to answer what they were asking me. I was not at all prepared or had any idea what the interview process would be like, I just went in blindly.

Performance and Perfection = Love and Worth

Let me tell you, pageant interviews can be some of the toughest interviews because you have no idea what they are going to ask. You have to be ready for anything. At least in a job interview they are probably going to ask you about your skills that make you good for the position. If you are an accountant, they will be asking you accounting questions, and, if you are a good accountant, you will be ready with those answers.

In pageantry, you never know what you are going to get. Political, personal, random, about anything goes, so you have to be very well prepared and on top of your game. It was truly a teaching moment that I will never forget and teach woman to this day. **Don't do anything or go into anything unprepared.** The problem was I didn't believe I could win nor did I really prepare.

Well, after that experience and not even making it into the top five, I knew that my thoughts about pageantry when I was little girl were true; I knew that it just wasn't for me. I had too many flaws, I wasn't smart enough, I was knock kneed and had an ugly scar on my leg, I wasn't pretty enough, and my family was not rich. I would never be perfect enough to be a pageant winner.

At the age of 24, I met another woman named Diane that would speak into my life and change it forever. Diane was from Georgia, where pageants are a huge deal. Her niece was in the Miss America pageant several years prior to our meeting, so she was from that world. It's funny because I met her at that same local pageant 5 years later.

The salon I worked in was in charge of doing hair and makeup for the contestants that year. My dear friend Tim, who was running the production, wanted me to meet this "new lady that moved into town". Because of her understanding of the pageant world, she was working with all the contestants on their walking and stage presence.

He walked me down to the room where Diane was doing some last minute prep work for the contestants. When I met her, the first thing she said to me in her cute southern draw was, "Why aren't you in this pageant?" She commented on how beautiful I was and how I should be doing pageants. She said I had "the look" for Miss USA and she challenged me to enter the Miss Ohio USA pageant. I explained to her that I had done a pageant when I was 18, and it just wasn't for me. I also was then engaged to be married.

Those women on television were in a league of their own and there was no way I could ever be one of them. Plus, I had already failed at one pageant. Diane taught me something different. She taught me a huge lesson that year: I could do anything I set my mind to, and nobody was better than me, nor was I better than anyone else. It was all about perception and preparation.

This was a new concept for me, I guess up until then I didn't realize we had the ability to change the direction of our lives. I didn't realize that we could actually play a role in it. I mean, I knew we made decisions about our lives like where to live, what career path to take and things like that. This was my first *real* experience with "personal growth" and how our thoughts affect us. Having some control over my life, going after what I wanted, and believing in my heart that I could do it. Not focusing on the other contestants and what they had, but rather focusing on myself and what I was there to do.

I remember stopping by my dad's to ask him what he thought about me competing and him being so excited and just interested in everything about it. We talked for a long time about the whole thing.

The weeks afterward, he would always bring it up every time I saw him. I was seeing a pattern. If I did something great, he was right there with me. I subconsciously was learning a huge misconception, that my worth was wrapped around my performances and accomplishments.

My dad is not a touchy-feely kind of guy, and definitely not an emotional guy. Never did I have that "daddy's little

Performance and Perfection = Love and Worth

girl" relationship with him; "I love you" or "I think you are amazing" were never in his vocabulary. Yet, in that moment, I remember just feeling like he loved me.

It always amazes me how much we crave our father's attention and love as little girls. Even though I had an amazing step dad, I just wanted my biological dad to love and adore me.

With Diane's belief in me and willingness to help coach me, I decided to give it a shot. We worked diligently on mastering interview skills, stage presence, and belief systems. She didn't realize it, but she was helping me not only win a pageant but helping me see things in a whole different light.

Thanks to Diane, I was prepared this time. I ended up winning Miss Ohio USA and got to compete in the nationally televised Miss USA pageant. That was huge for me! I felt like I was earning everyone's love and finding my worth. I was also learning all about personal growth and believing in yourself.

I also had the confidence to end my engagement. I knew deep down I didn't want to marry him but it just felt like it was the natural next step since we had dated for so long. I had prayed for a long time for God to give me a way out and I promised Him if He did I would take it. This was my way out.

Several years later in 1991 I married my wonderful husband, Don, and we had our first 2 children by 1996. A few years later I had the opportunity to compete in the Mrs. Ohio pageant. I was very excited because 50% of your score was interview and platform—what you wanted to advocate during your year reign. Mine of course would be diabetes awareness.

You see my husband was a type-one diabetic, and I had been studying the disease for years. We had become very involved with fundraising, and I loved teaching people about the disease. It had been my goal to become a national spokesperson for *The American Diabetes Association*. I was truly passionate about my platform of diabetes because I lived it, and I knew I could help other families who struggled with this disease.

Back then, you had to go to the library and look through the card catalog to see if they had a book. This was before you could just look online and search it. I went to the library to see if I could find a children's book to read to my little girls to help them understand diabetes. I wanted to make sure that if something happened to their dad while I was away that they knew to call 911 and tell them their daddy is a diabetic. I knew reading them a fun children's book about it would help them remember and keep it light.

I found absolutely nothing on this topic, so I took it upon myself to write a book and read it to the girls to help them understand diabetes the best way a young child could.

I knew if I could get it published, it would help thousands of others who are dealing with the same issues. However, back then the only way I knew to get a book published was through a traditional publisher and I knew NOTHING about that.

What I did know about were pageants, and I saw this as my vehicle to achieve my goal. If I could win Mrs. Ohio with diabetes as my platform, it would give me the resources and vehicle to get my book published. If I could do this, I would really feel worthy because I would be able to help others.

I won Mrs. Ohio International! My new director, Susan, was an amazing woman who had a **huge** impact on my life (and still does to this day). With her help I went on to win the international competition and became Mrs. International. I became the national spokesperson for the American Diabetes Association and traveled all over the United States. I also worked with an international pharmaceutical company speaking to doctors from all over the world about the importance of patient education. They even published my book and distributed it all over the country to help families just like ours.

Performance and Perfection = Love and Worth

This was an amazing time in my life and I thought I was definitely defining my worth. It was all because I was "beautiful" and a title holder that all of these wonderful things were happening for me **(another misconception).**

After all the excitement of over 3 years competing, winning, and speaking, it all came to a dead stop when it was over. I felt this emptiness in my soul that I wasn't worthy enough because I was not doing anything fabulous to earn anyone's love. My marriage started to suffer.

We had worked very hard to put my husband through college. He had worked hard to get not only his bachelor's degree but his master's degree as well. He wanted to further his education so he could move up in the corporate world and better provide for our family.

At this time, he had gotten a job in Columbus, which was about a 60-minute commute from our home if there was no traffic. He was gone a lot while I was home with the girls and working, all while living with my feeling of unworthiness and inadequacy. It really started causing problems for us. I was feeling alone and overwhelmed with doing everything at home while he was always away. We were both giving it everything we had to get him through school. I began to pray, and pray hard, for help from God to save my marriage. And little by little we worked to get our marriage back on track.

My husband and I started going to church together for the first time in our marriage and I rededicated my life to God, but the same old Lisa showed up for this round with God too. Being that I have the personality that when I decide to do something, I am going to be the best at whatever it is, I was going to be the best Christian and earn God's love. It felt like the same treadmill I had been on my entire life. What could I do to earn someone's love? How could I do it the perfect way?

We went to church every Sunday and got very involved. I felt like I was trying to get a college education in a very short amount of time when it came to "religion." At the time, we were going to a very charismatic church, and I was so on fire to learn everything that I could, and my journey to become a great Christian was well underway.

The more I learned, the more I didn't understand why everyone else did things differently. I passed a lot of judgment towards people ("religion" will do that to you). I wanted to do everything right so God would love me—and maybe, just maybe, my life would have meaning and be fulfilling.

But here is the catch—I am getting older and my outer youth and beauty are fading, and I can no longer use it to do all these fabulous things to earn God's love. I guess I had always associated me being pretty and the attention it brought to me with being worthy of love, now how was that going to work when my outer appearance was aging?

I worked hard over the next several years at earning God's love. My husband became the head of children's ministry at church so I thought I got bonus points for that one; I had 2 more children and became a stay at home mom. I worked diligently at keeping my house tidy, started my own business from home, worked as a spokesperson for Juvenile Diabetes, became a health and wellness expert and advocate, won many business awards, and life continued on the same path—working at something to gain the love of God and others.

After several years I found myself in a hole, a pit to which I just could not get out. When my youngest son started to school and all 4 of my children were in school all day, I started struggling with whom I was and what I was supposed to be doing with my life. I internalized my feelings and kept pushing through.

Performance and Perfection = Love and Worth

I have always been that person that motivates and inspires people to get healthy, to live life, to go after their dreams and goals, and I suddenly found myself to have none of my own.

I was the friend that everyone came to with their problems and issues. Yet I only had a friend or two that I could truly talk to. But even then I was very guarded so I wouldn't seem weak. I kept sinking further and further into my hole, and, as I always tell others, the more you focus on something the bigger it becomes—and, boy did I find that to be true.

For over 2 years I had this internal struggle, and no matter what I did, no matter how much I tried to "do" to get out of it, I remained in that place. I bought countless self-help books, daily devotionals, online courses, anything that I thought I could accomplish to finally have God be pleased with me. I was trying once again to do something to earn my way out of this mess and to earn His love, but nothing was happening.

I was praying for God to give me some meaning for my life, and I was open to whatever He wanted for me: a job, a volunteer position, any opportunity that He wanted me to do. I waited for an answer, but nothing. Nothing ever came to me. What could I possibly DO to make this happen, to make God love me enough to want this for me?

I remember one morning being in my bedroom all by myself and I felt this anger just build up inside of me. I just got really angry at God and was on my knees yelling at him. "What do you want from me, what do you want me to do? I have told you I am open to your will, whatever direction you want me to go and yet you give me NOTHING!!!" I yelled; I cried; then I pulled myself together quickly, like I always do, and I went about my day.

Have you ever felt that way? Just a feeling of inadequacy, lack, not enough? You just want to "do" or "be" something to be accepted or loved. You think that perfectionism is somehow attainable. Trust me when I say there is a difference between perfection and greatness. While the quest to perfection can lead to constantly feeling inadequate—or "not good enough"—greatness is a journey taken when you are seeking to become a better version of yourself.

NEWS FLASH—there is no perfect, and in trying to pursue perfection, we are missing out on so much life has to offer. We are living a lie.

I had to learn, and still remind myself of this every day, to just enjoy the journey. To relax and let go of the uptight things I had a tendency to hold on to. I had to learn to stop trying to work for everyone's acceptance and love because, let's be real here, you are never going to be accepted and loved by everyone.

I had to learn to love myself! Rob Liano said, "Self-respect, self-worth and self-love, all start with self. Stop looking outside of yourself for your value." I had to do some deep reflection. I had to learn that I can perform and be on stage because I truly love it and not because of any other reason. I had to learn that I love competition of all kinds and that's okay, it's just how I am wired.

I had to learn that I am ENOUGH! I am worthy of love even when I am in a funk with no goals, sitting on my couch, watching daytime television, and feeling sorry for myself and angry with God. I am worthy of love when I do a talk to 1,000 people about nutrition and the importance of taking care of themselves, and when I am just showing love to my children. I am worthy of love when I write a book, and when I'm watching my favorite TV show.

I am learning and will continue to learn this every day because we are always learning and evolving into what God has set out for our lives. And I know I will have times when I fall back into old ways of thinking, but I will continue to think of this time in my life and what I learned, and I will work through it knowing I am loved.

Your Crowning Moment

It's Time To Move On

This is when I am going to really get "real" with you. Yes, I had things happen in my life that made me feel the way I did, and they did have a hand in molding me into feeling certain ways about things. I spent a lot of time in my life blaming the way I was or how I felt with different things in my younger years.

Though they did mold me and affect me, they don't control me. I am not here to spend a lot of time and energy telling you the psychology behind it all. I spent a lot of time in my life working so hard to make people like me. It was like I was walking around carrying a neon sign that said "PLEASE LIKE ME." This is what I have learned, and I want you to hear. Our past is just that, our past! EVERYTHING that we have gone through in life is for a bigger purpose than we will ever comprehend. As soon as we can grasp hold of that, and stop rolling in the muck of the past, we can move forward into our future.

It is so hard to move forward when you have so much attachment to the past. Each person remembers the past in a way that is significant to them and how they perceived it. A lot of times it is a misconception, but it is the way we personally saw it. Make sense?

Even people that had seemingly normal childhoods still find things that affect them as they get older. Parents, siblings, friends, teachers, poor, rich, the list goes on and on. I think it is just human nature for some people to try and figure out or place blame on things they can't figure out or understand.

You *cannot* change the past, nor can you fix it, so the best thing you can do is to leave it in the past. This means leaving all the things that happened to you growing up in the past as well. Those things happened and made you who you are at this moment but they don't have to define who you will be in the future.

I know many people who had terrible childhoods and still hang onto the hurt, pain, and disappointment they experienced. It is not a good place to live at all. It keeps you from the joy of life. Stop letting what happened in the past define who you are now.

I held on for years that I had to earn people's love, and it got me nowhere but disappointment and never feeling enough. I can never do enough to get everyone to like me, all I can do is like me! I will disappoint people and people will disappoint me, but as soon as I grasped ahold of that concept, it was very freeing! Now I love people for who they are and I'm okay if that feeling is not reciprocated.

I hear people tell me all the time that someone hurt them deeply. They are so consumed with that hurt and hatred towards that other person that it can rule their life. What I try to explain to them is that they are spending all this time and energy being angry with someone and letting that person continue to have power over their life. The sad part is that usually while they are feeling all the anger and hurt, the other person has moved on and not given it a second thought. All of the energy you are spending in that negative space is worthless.

Forgiveness is not always about others, but about our own spiritual growth. We have to forgive and let go for ourselves so we can move on into our future.

To those of you that feel unworthy, not good enough, undeserving, unsatisfied in who you are or how you look, bored with life, feeling hopeless, overwhelmed, unhappy—every man and woman, young or old—for anyone that can relate to this story in anyway, YOU are enough!

If you are a single mom working three jobs to make ends meet or if you have done things in your past that you are not proud of, you are worthy of love.

There is a great quote from Buddha that says, *"You can search throughout the entire universe for someone who is more deserving of your love and affection than you are yourself, and that person is not to be found anywhere. You yourself, as much as anybody in the entire universe deserve your love and affection."*

Performance and Perfection = Love and Worth

No matter what you've been through in your life, you deserve unconditional self-love. All of the struggles and challenges that you have fought against and the "mistakes" that you feel you've made are all for a much grander purpose than you are able to see. You are still enough despite all of it. We are all a work in progress and we have to learn to be gracious with ourselves.

Stop searching for approval from everyone else. Set goals for yourself to make yourself proud.

Make a list of what make you happy. Some of these things could be as simple as wearing red lipstick, wearing pants instead of a skirt to work, dancing around in the living room, singing in the shower, going for long walks, or even having the windows down on your drive home.

Next make a list of things that you do every day—laundry, making dinner for your family, etc.

Lastly, make a list of things you do because of other people. Perhaps it's spending 30 minutes on your make-up in the mornings even though you hate wearing make-up, only wearing clothes that you think will impress others but you feel are uncomfortable, or maybe saying yes to things that you really don't want or don't have time to do.

Compare these lists. What things do you have on the first list that are missing from the second one? What things can you add to your day to make you happy? What are some things on the last list that you can change or do away with all together? We often do things for other peoples' approval before we do things for ourselves. Perhaps you see it as a "selfless" action, when it actually can be self-destructing. Rather than seeking approval from everyone else, start doing things for yourself.

That's me in the white sweater when I had tons of self-esteem and "leadership skills".

My first pageant (4th from the right in black)

Winning Miss Ohio USA at the age of 24 years old.

With my mom and step-dad, Sue and Perry.

My love for performing was obvious when I got to perform on the Miss USA stage.

Winning Mrs. International

MISS CONCEPTION #2

If I Looked a Certain Way, I Would Be Happy

At about the age of 18, I started working on being and staying skinny. That was the word that was used back in the 70's and 80's—SKINNY!! Years later, I started working on being healthy and strong. There's a big difference, and I'm sure many of you can relate to my story.

This journey has probably been the biggest **"Misconception"** of my life—the quest to have the perfect body, or what I thought was the perfect body. What you should know is that I am not a naturally thin girl. My mom, dad, sister, brother, aunts, uncles, and cousins all have struggled with their weight for as long as I can remember.

As a young girl, I don't remember being obsessed with my weight. As a matter fact, I can remember my girlfriend and I always getting an extra-large pizza, eating it, and watching MTV as young teenagers and never gave it a second thought.

I remember one of my best friend and I would always go to this restaurant in our town, a little local place that had these huge sandwiches. We would each get a large fry and top it off with this huge Reese's Pieces sundae (when I say huge, I mean HUGE! Something I would probably bring to the table for a family of four). But eating to me was just fun, as I'm sure it is to millions of teenagers. And at that time in our lives, we really never worry about it because we are so active.

Boy, when I think back to that time I sure do miss it! Not focused on weight, what I ate or how I looked; wouldn't it be nice to live in that space all your life?

I can remember when I first really started focusing on weight. I was a senior in high school in the early 80s. I had always been a cheerleader and very active. We practiced all the time, all summer and all during the school year. But I remember after football season of my senior year things beginning to change with my body.

Cheerleading was over, and I was doing nothing. I had a car now so I wasn't riding my bike. No more cheer practice, no more bike riding, no more gymnastics. Things were just different now.

I felt my body starting to change. For the first time, I remember just not feeling right, not feeling good about my body. I went from never giving it a second thought, to all of the sudden feeling very aware of my body and how "fat" I was feeling. It was like a switch went off in my head. And it was a switch that has never been completely turned off. Can you relate to this at all?

I remember hearing the word anorexia for the very first time my senior year of high school. A girl in my class was away at a rehabilitation hospital of some kind, and the rumors around the school were going crazy. Nobody had ever heard of this disease before, and I remember sitting at the lunch table with a group of my friends talking about what it was. One girl told us how "Mary" would go to the restroom after she ate any food and throw it up.

This was foreign to all of us girls but I remember a couple of my friends thought it was just a fabulous idea! So after lunch they would go into the restroom and do the same. It was just kind of a novelty thing, and I wasn't about to do it at school. I do remember trying it a few times myself at home, and trust me, in the beginning it was awful! I didn't understand how anyone could do something like that all the time. I hated throwing up. *This was the dumbest thing anyone could have come up with*, I thought. So that is when I decided I would do a "real" diet!

Growing up, I never worried about my weight at all. However, what I do remember is that my mom was always on a diet. I have memories of walking into the kitchen, and it smelling really awful, and I knew when I smelled that smell that my mom was on a diet. For some reason she always would have canned spinach when she was attempting to lose weight, and trust me when I say the smell is not great. I love fresh spinach today, but I can still remember that smell. I'm sure there are very few kids that would like the smell of canned spinach!

There were many more diets along the way. Some of the other diets I remember my mom doing are the cabbage soup diet, wearing some kind of clip on her ear that was supposed to help with her appetite, going to a hypnotist, some kind of chewing gum diet, and the one that really sticks out in my mind—the Beverly Hills Diet.

I was a little bit older at this point, probably my early teens, and we went on a really fun trip in a motorhome. I remember we were at the campground. I believe that my mom's watermelon and grape day was the next morning, so we all walked probably half a mile down to a grocery store so that my mom could get all of her fruit for the next day.

For those of you that are not familiar with the Beverly Hills diet, it was where you would eat fruit in different combinations all day, every day. Knowing what I know now, it's craziness! But back then, I guess it worked for some. Like I always say, diets work, it's just can you live that way the rest of your life?

I also remember my mom had a scale with her on the motorhome and she would get on the scale and weigh herself and was so excited that her weight was dropping. Those are all the things that I remember when I was young. And believe me, there have been many, many more weight-loss attempts by my mom, aunt, and friends since that time.

I say all that because I thought I knew a lot about diets, so at this point is when I came up with my own diet. The first diet I, Lisa Moser, was ever on was one I called the "suck-on-candy-all-day-long diet". Yes, that's exactly what I did. I would get up and go to school, not eat breakfast, and have hard candy in my purse. I would literally suck on hard candy all day long. Then I would come home and I would lay on the couch and take a nap. I guess that happens when you've been eating candy and then crashing all day long—by the time you get home you just want to sleep.

So I would take a nap, and then when my parents would get home my mom would make dinner, and I would allow myself that one meal and that was it. Then I would just do it all over again the next day.

I remember doing all this leading up to my senior prom and I really did feel good about myself physically. I had a lot of friends commenting on how much weight I lost and how good I looked. It was the beginning of one of my biggest misconceptions of my life. I always say everybody's first diet, no matter what it is, you're going to drop weight quickly because your body has never experienced it before. But as many of you know, as we get older and do it over and over and over and over again, it gets more difficult.

I then graduated from high school, and my life was about to change. I had decided that I wanted to become a cosmetologist and work in the salon my mom owned. I loved fashion and grew up in the salon, so it just felt like a natural transition for me.

I was going to move away in the fall and go to beauty school. I don't remember feeling any real anxiety about it. But I was very close to my family, so I knew it would not be an easy transition. This would literally be my first time away from my family. I think the only thing I had ever done to be away from home was cheerleading camp every summer.

This is the summer when my thought process around my body image and how I felt about myself all changed. I needed to take control of the food that I ate. I needed to be thin and beautiful.

I know now as an adult, I was also trying to control my life because as an 18-year-old moving away you feel like you're losing control over your life and what you know. So I became obsessed with what I ate, I would deprive myself of food, and I would eat very low calorie meals. I wrote everything down that went in my mouth and could literally tell you the calorie count of every food on the planet at that time in my life.

Then I started to really get obsessed. I started trying to do what I had learned about my senior year of high school. I started throwing up after I would eat. Honestly as I write this I can still remember what it felt like to be totally obsessed 24 hours a day, seven days a week with everything that I ate and put into my body.

I can remember going home on the weekends, walking into the house, and my parents not being there. I would sit on the floor in the kitchen in front of the cereal cabinet and just eat frosted flakes, unable to stop. That's when I would start the binging.

Binging is what I would do after days and days of limiting my calorie intake. I learned so much about my body and why things happened to me during my journey but I'm not going to get into the psychology of why this was happening. Nor will I get into the physical things that were happening to my body, as I'm not a doctor, and this is not a book about anorexia or bulimia. (visit www.LisaMoser.com for more information on my wellness program) But it is a book about "**misconceptions**".

This has been one of the biggest misconceptions of my life. I desperately want to help others going through anything similar, the valuable lessons I have learned in my years of struggles. My hope is that I can help people by sharing my story and what I have learned.

For those that knew me, I was tall, pretty, had an amazing family, and I had my own apartment at school in Columbus, Ohio. How cool was that! Little did people know that I was so unhappy on the inside because all I did 24 hours a day/7

days a week was focus on food and my body image. Everything that I did, every party I went to, every date I went on, it all revolved around what I was going to eat (or not eat) and if I was going to purge when I got home. It was awful.

I can remember after going out to dinner with friends or a boyfriend, walking to my bedroom, and either walking straight into my bedroom or turning left into the bathroom. The fight in my head that I would have all the time trying to tell myself to just go to bed. "The food wasn't going to hurt me, it was fine!" But 90% of the time, I would turn, go in the restroom, and get rid of the food because I would feel so much better getting rid of the guilt.

I struggled with this for quite some time, probably about four to five years. Nobody really knew about it, and I could honestly write hundreds of pages on some of the things that I did and how I would hide it, but I think you get the idea. What I really want you to understand is that this was such an obsession for me, it was a big misconception.

I put so much time and effort and emphasis on looking perfect and being a certain weight. I thought once I got there I would be happy and everything would be perfect. If I just looked like the models on TV or the Miss USA contestants, then it would all be perfect, and I would be happy! And I was only in my early 20s. Nobody knew! Everyone thought that I just had it all.

Let's talk about this journey into pageantry and what it really looked like for me. In the previous chapter I talked about how I got to the Miss USA stage. I talked about how I always watched pageants on television and never in a million years thought I could ever be on that stage. It wasn't even a dream of mine at the time. But I shared with you how that vision changed.

If I Looked a Certain Way, I Would Be Happy

I found myself on a stage in Columbus, Ohio competing for the title of Miss Ohio USA, it was so hard to even imagine that I was there. Way over a hundred girls competing for the title that year and I was the new girl. The new girl that had never been there before, nor had I won any previous pageants when I was younger. Nobody really payed any attention to me, and the returning girls that were highly competitive never even saw me as competition.

I **was** competition. And when they announced my name as the winner it was like a dream. I got whisked away to sign all the legal documents, paperwork, and to do all the news media coverage. I felt like I was about to embark on something really big. I don't want to take this chapter to get in to all the stories about the pageant and everything that led up to me being on the Miss USA stage, but instead I want to take this time to show you the big *misconception* of what people saw, as to what I felt.

Here is the image of what people saw, the misconception so to speak. I was a 24-year-old, 5'9, thin, pretty girl that was on the Miss USA stage. I was competing against women from all over the United States who had won the same competition in their state. And I was considered one of the prettiest woman in the United States!

I looked happy, excited, and overjoyed to be there. I looked like I had it all together. Thanks to my mom and stepdad, I had everything I needed to be there and compete and feel good about myself and the way I looked, but on the inside there was something different going on.

Since I had struggled with my body image and dieting and eating disorders for several years, this was a really stressful situation to be in. I had worked really hard in the past few years to get my eating disorder under control. I had discovered that exercise was kind of my savior. I worked really hard trying to watch what I ate and at that time, counting calories was really a big thing. I worked to keep my calorie count at what

I thought was good for me. But at this time in my life I still did not have a good relationship with food. It was just that I was able to eat it and not go to the bathroom to throw it up.

Food was still on my mind 24 hours a day, seven days a week. So what people saw was this put together, tall, beautiful girl competing in the Miss USA Pageant; what they didn't see was the turmoil and internal fight I had going on in my own head about the way I looked.

What they also didn't know was that because of my eating disorder and not feeding my body nutritionally what it needed, I ended up with a huge chemical imbalance. So for almost a year I had been taking an antidepressant.

Let's think about this huge **misconception** of what people saw and what was actually going on. I hope this helps you understand that not everything is as it seems; we can't always wish we had what somebody else has.

To have all of this going on in my mind about how I felt about my body, being on the Miss USA stage was probably not the best place for me. Let me fill you in on a typical week in the Miss USA pageant competition. Let me just say, when I competed, it was the first year that Procter & Gamble owned the Miss USA system, and I believe it was the only year that they had the contestants come for one entire month.

I left my home in Ohio and I had to go to Mobile, Alabama and compete for four weeks. Now for someone that has a relationship with food the way I did, this could be challenging to be away from home and my routine and not in total control of the environment. BUT, you figure since it's a bunch of pageant girls, they're probably going to feed you salad and have food like that around and give you time to workout, so it would make it a lot easier. Oh how wrong I was. They really rolled out the red carpet for us!

Every morning we would get up and we would go down to breakfast and have this spread of food that was beyond anything I've ever seen. I always heard about southern cooking and, boy, did we get to experience it that month. It was beautiful and amazing and it was every single morning.

Then we had rehearsal after breakfast. We would go to the rehearsal hall, and they would have tables set up with so-called "snacks" for us—they had every kind of goodie you can imagine there while we were at rehearsal. I'm not sure why since we literally just ate, but it seemed like it was in the contract that they had to have food available to us at all times.

We would then leave and go to lunch, which was usually at some phenomenal local restaurant that wanted to host the Miss USA contestants in their establishment. The places that we went to eat were absolutely amazing.

When we were back at rehearsal there was food there again, and then dinner was a huge event. We had big galas or some kind of fundraising event or military dinners. I could go on and on about all the amazing, fabulous things that we got to do, and the amazing people we got to meet. But for me, every single thing we did, my focus was around the food and what I could and couldn't eat.

Amazing, phenomenal, wonderful food; it was absolutely mind-boggling.

I remember one day after breakfast, 15 or so of the contestants that could sing were chosen to go to a recording studio to record the singing for the opening number. The goal was to make it sound like all fifty women were singing on television. We had a police escorted bus that took us to the recording studio where we were only going to be for an hour or so.

When we walked into the recording studio, what do you think was along the wall waiting for us—a gorgeous buffet of snacks in case we got hungry while we were recording. Seriously? These are pageant girls. These are women who have worked there butts off (literally) for months to be in the best shape of their life to compete, yet they're following us around with food. I think they would have saved thousands and thousands of dollars if they had someone in charge of the food schedule that understood competition.

I tell you all of this because, for most, that would have been the coolest experience—to be able to eat different foods and go to different restaurants that you would never otherwise get to experience. It would have been so amazing.

Someone with my mindset, someone where food is the enemy—one of your demons that you have been fighting against for years—this was a really, really hard place to be. I can remember working so hard just to eat as healthy as I possibly could.

It wasn't like it is now, where you can ask for healthier options or for them to make things specifically for you. And, this was the South. To this day I have yet to find a piece of key-lime pie that even comes close to what I ate in Mobile, Alabama. If you live there and want to send me a piece, I would happily eat it with a big smile on my face today.

And forget about working out, there was never time scheduled in the day for that. Most girls would run the halls of the hotel in the evenings or in the lobby during a break. I would jump on my bed in the evenings to get some cardio work in for the day.

So what looked like the most amazing time in my life; looked like an opportunity of a lifetime; seemed like something that most girls could only dream of; people thinking that I literally had it all—that was the **misconception**!!

I was struggling every single day I was there with this maddening perception about how I had to look a certain way. I had to have this perfect body that, honestly, I don't know what that was supposed to look like. Especially now when I look back at pictures. What was it that I didn't like?

It is amazing how we do let our minds rule how we feel about ourselves and about situations and we don't just allow ourselves to live in the moment. As I write this, I cry tears for that young girl that was bullying herself so badly that she missed out on an experience of a lifetime—that she was so deep into her own misconception of what she thought she was supposed to look like and feel. I don't want any young girl or woman of any age feel that way about herself ever.

Don't let your mind bully you! If I could tell my younger self one thing of importance about this subject, it would be to understand that you cannot live peacefully in your body if your mind is constantly at war with you.

How we talk to ourselves is a very powerful thing. That was exactly what was happening to me when this all began when I was a teenager. All of a sudden my mind started telling me that my body wasn't perfect—that something was wrong. I wasn't the "ideal" that everyone expected of me or what I saw in magazines or on television. My mind started playing tricks with me when I was looking in the mirror.

As I'm sure many of you can relate, I will look back at pictures to this day of when I was young and wonder what the heck I was so unhappy with. But our minds can be our biggest enemy, and when we start feeding our thoughts more and more negative information, we start believing it. We get dissatisfied, critical, sad, and depressed and we lose our joy.

I lived the majority of my younger life with a lack of joy—joy that was taken from me by myself, from my own thoughts, and the way that I saw myself. No matter what your age, if I could tell you one thing, it is this message: **"Don't let your mind bully you."**

We as women have enough going against us with the bombardment of social media pictures, photos in magazines, models, commercials, TV personalities, and entertainers all telling us to wear a certain thing, to look a certain way, and to be a certain size.

Bullying in schools is getting so much attention right now because it has gotten out of hand with social media. Just today

I saw on Facebook where a young girl shot herself in front of her family because she was being bullied for years at school and on social media. My heart broke when I read that, and I can only imagine what this young woman was feeling and how awful she thought things were in her mind to do something to this caliber. I just pray that this madness stops.

I love what Selena Gomez said at the American Music Awards. She was giving her speech and talked about how she "had it all but was broken on the inside." I relate to that. She also said, "I don't want to see your bodies on Instagram. I want to see what's in here," pointing to her heart. She said she's not trying to get validation nor does she need it anymore. That's the place where we all need to get, and I applaud this young, beautiful woman for understanding that at such a young age and sharing that message with the world!

So how do you begin? How do you begin to stop letting your mind bully you and start believing you are amazing?

For me personally, it came down to self-talk. It came down to changing my believe system when it came to food, why I eat food, my body image, and how I saw myself.

Let's start with self-talk. What do you say to yourself when you get up in the morning and you look in the mirror? What do you say to yourself when you get dressed for the day and you are ready to go but maybe just don't feel your best? What do you say to yourself when you just don't feel like you're enough? How about when you are getting dressed in the morning and look at herself in the mirror? Do you start by telling yourself how bad you look?

Usually we all start picking on parts of our bodies that we don't like. Maybe we feel our thighs are too thick, our arms are too flabby, or our butt is too big. Or how about wishing we could get rid of our belly?

There are so many different things that we can look at ourselves in the mirror and we automatically go to those

If I Looked a Certain Way, I Would Be Happy

negative things and thoughts in our head. All we are doing is picking on things that we don't think are perfect and wishing we could change about ourselves. That is right where our minds go every single time we look at ourselves in the mirror and that is what we keep telling ourselves every single time we look in the mirror.

Then we get so good at criticizing ourselves that we don't even have to look at ourselves in the mirror to tear ourselves down. We can just be walking and think about our size or how we are too short, or how our jeans don't fit the way we want.

We tear ourselves down when someone gives us a compliment. If a friend says you look really pretty today, we have a hard time just saying "thank you." Women have a tendency to want to negate everything that they were just told by their friend in that compliment. *"You look great in those jeans, I love them"* is responded with a *"oh no I don't, these jeans make me look so fat."* Then a *"you look really pretty today. I like the way you did your make up,"* is given the response of *"are you kidding me, I didn't even do my makeup very well this morning and I need to get a haircut."* You are even putting down your hair and they never even mentioned your hair!! You are making sure they see how awful you are! *"You look so cute in that outfit"* is followed by an *"oh my gosh I have gained so much weight. I feel so fat."*

We have gotten to a place where we can't even accept a compliment from anyone. We get uncomfortable excepting a nice comment about ourselves. And then if you're really bad like I was when I was younger, I would write in a journal every day about how I felt so terrible about my body and what I ate that day and how many calories I had and how much exercise I did or didn't do that day. I would focus on the negative and put it in writing!! And the more we focus on something the bigger it gets in our minds. Then we get really good at bullying ourselves.

We have got to stop the cycle. We have got to learn to build each other up. More importantly we have to learn to build ourselves up.

There is a huge platform on women building up other women, but it's got to start with ourselves. We have to build ourselves up before anybody else can build us up.

Your Crowning Moment

Change your thoughts,
Change your world.
—Norman Vincent Peale

The hard part about self-talk is that it always feels true. Even though your negative thoughts our often incorrect, you tend to assume that they are facts. You can learn to notice your negative self-talk as it happens and CHOOSE to think in a more positive way. It will just take time and practice, but it will be worth it—and believe me, once you start focusing on what you are saying, you will be surprised at how much your thinking is exaggerated or focused on the negative in whatever situation you are facing.

Our actions are inspired by our thoughts. So if we can begin to change the way we think then we can begin to change the way we feel. Now this will take some work if you have a long history of negative self-talk. It didn't begin overnight so it's not going to go away overnight.

The following are some steps to take to get you started on your way to positive self-talk:

1. ***Envision what it's like to be a confident you***

A great way to start is to create an image of yourself as the confident and self-assured person you aspire to become. How does it feel to be this person? How will others perceive you? What does your body language look like? How do you come across to others? Close your eyes and see these things clearly in your mind. Experience being and seeing things from that person's perspective. Practice doing this every morning. I practice this still to this day if I am going somewhere that I know will be uncomfortable or uneasy for me. I get into this head space and walk into that room confident in who I am!

The opinion you have of yourself is the most important opinion you have. You are constantly conveying what you are feeling on the inside. If you feel unattractive on the inside, you can be the most beautiful person in the world who will be convey feelings of unattractiveness, and it will push people away.

The problem is on the inside. You carry yourself the way you see yourself. Haven't you witnessed that yourself? Have you ever known a guy that you didn't feel was the most attractive thing you've ever seen, BUT he is so sure of himself? He is an amazing person; he's kind, generous, a great heart, confident, secure, and all of the sudden, you see him in a total different way. "Oh he has the cutest smile. I adore his crooked nose."

What's the difference? On the inside he sees himself as strong, talented, gifted and extremely confident. What's on the inside eventually will show up on the outside. The key here is people tend to see you the way you see you. You carry yourself the way you see yourself!

2. ***Don't compare yourself to others.***

It's so easy to measure your worth against other people. Find what you are good at and keep your focus on you not others. You will always be able to find someone that has accomplished something you wish you could have accomplished or has something you wish you could have. If you are constantly doing this, you will always be on the losing end of that one.

Begin embracing your uniqueness and your accomplishments. Start creating your own goals and personal and/or professional development plan. Work towards being the best YOU and stop worrying about everyone else.

3. ***Positive reinforcement***

Stop building negative thought upon negative thought. It is time to start telling yourself some positive affirmations. Start small with very focused statements. Things like:

- -I am enough.
- -I am healthy and happy.
- -I am more than my appearance.

-I am a good person.
-I can get through anything.
-I am loved.
-I am loyal.
-Today will be my day.
-I am prosperous.
-I am happy.
-I am healthy.
-I have special qualities.
-I am confident.
-I can do anything I put my mind to.
-I love myself.

"Never say anything about yourself you do not want to come true!"
—Rick Godwin

Repeat these to yourself every day when you start to go to the negative side of something. Catch yourself in the act and switch it up! Say them with true feeling and emotions, don't just read them. Get them into your very being and soon you will start to believe them. Like I said, this isn't going to happen overnight, but keep at it and I promise you will begin to see little things start to change.

4. *Surround yourself with positive influences.*

It is so important to identify those negative factors in our lives which may be helping keep us in this negative space. Negative friends can be the worst and feed into your own negative self-talk. They can especially be toxic when you are working hard to change your thoughts and action. You will find yourself taking one step forward and then 3 steps back.
It is so important to surround yourself with positive people who empower you. You will begin to feel uplifted

and have a desire for more personal growth. People will either inspire you, or they will drain you.

You cannot expect positive changes in your life if you are surrounding yourself with negative people.

Find a mentor. I work with women every day to encourage and help lift up and inspire them to be their best self. Everyone needs someone! I have a few of my own and I honestly don't know what I would do without them. Find those people in your life!

Footnote: If you are struggling with your body image and just don't like what you see in the mirror, positive self-talk is the way to begin. You have to change your thoughts and actions around your body and your relationship with food.

I'm not a doctor, registered dietitian, or a therapist who works with eating disorders. All I can share with you is my experience. I write this with the hope that I can help people have a better understanding so that they may not have to go through the years and years of struggle like I did. What I really just want to share with you and what it all boils down to is working really hard to get a better understanding of food and how it affects your body. My life began to change when I started figuring this piece of the puzzle out.

Why do you think there are thousands and thousands of different diets out? Some work for some people and not for others. Low-carb, high-protein, exercise plans, low calorie counting, macronutrients counting, high glycemic… I could go on and on with all the different things over the years that people have used to try to lose weight so that they can so-called "feel better" about themselves.

Have you heard people say "food is like a drug?" You'll hear that from people who have food addictions and they'll tell you that food is like a drug that helps them cope. Food was a drug for me when I would be sitting in front of that cupboard eating cereal uncontrollably because I had deprived my body of calories all week. Food was like a drug when all I did was think about it 24 hours a day, seven days a week.

What I try to teach people is an understanding of how food affects us in a positive way. How we need to learn to eat and feed our bodies for energy and for our health. We need to begin to understand how foods are affecting us and the way we feel, our moods, highs and lows, the crashing, energy levels. If everyone could learn just small steps on eating healthy and how that impacts our body not just physically but mentally as well, I am sure we would start taking those steps.

I have a true passion for educating people on that very understanding because it comes from my heart. It comes from me living in a place for many, many years where I did not understand this concept. All I did was try to lose weight to become a certain weight or something, and I thought that was going to make me happy. What I didn't understand at the time was with all the food depravation, all of the weird diets, all of the failed attempts, were making me more miserable and more unhappy, and my body was not loving it.

I am still learning new things all the time. I have a true passion for educating myself on health and wellness and fitness. I want to be healthy and fit and happy for many, many years to come but it takes work and dedication and doing things a little bit differently than society today teaches us.

One of my favorite things is working with people to do just that. Several years ago I developed a health and wellness program that was used in schools systems, businesses, groups and individuals all over the United States. It was a six-week program that helps people understand food and how it affects our bodies in simple steps. I could write a separate book on all of that information alone. If you're interested in learning more about the program you can visit my website www.LisaMoser.com.

My message in this section is to please stop the madness! Start talking to yourself in a positive way and stop focusing on all of your so-called flaws. We all have them. Nobody is perfect! If you want to lose weight and you don't like how you feel, than do it because you have the power to do it! Just do it the right way. Start the process because you want to look and feel your best.... YOUR best! Not what the media tell you is your best.

Don't do it to look a certain way for somebody or because society is telling you that you need to look a certain way. You want to feel more energy and be healthy. If you know you don't eat healthy and it's not good for you then do something about it.

Step up into a new direction, a new way of thinking. Find that mentor that can help you. Talk to yourself in a positive way every day. Tell yourself that you're fabulous and that you can do anything you set your mind to do.

You've got this! Don't live in that negative space. Let's start living in a place of joy!

Looking back at this photo I wonder what it was about my body I was so unhappy about?

Send-off to Miss USA

Filming on the beach at Miss USA

Feeling really insecure beside this beauty in a photo shoot.

Miss USA bathing suit competition (3rd on the right)

MISS CONCEPTION #3

FEAR
Stories We Tell Ourselves

Helene Lerner once wrote,

> *Fear can prevent us from achieving great heights of success by distorting reality or being grounded in false beliefs. Stepping up and taking action allows us to move through those fears. However, taking action itself can foster fear by pushing us outside our comfort zone. But that's okay because being challenged means we're growing. Confidence doesn't require fearlessness, rather the ability to step into uncharted territory and get comfortable with the uncomfortable."*

Have you ever felt like fear of something held you back? **Fear has a way of putting detour signs up in our life's journey**. I'm not talking about a-bear-running-towards-you-in-the-woods kind of fear, but the mind controlling fear that holds our thoughts hostage. I have let fear make so many decisions in my life that I will never know what could have come from me saying "YES" instead of "I can't." All I do know is I always sit and wonder "what if I had tried? What if I had taken that path?" The "what if's" are no fun at all.

There are a lot of decisions that we make in life that we don't always like, but we know we're making the right decision. You feel peace about it even though you may not like the decision you had to make.

Then there are those life altering decisions. The ones that drive you crazy thinking about them. Is it a good opportunity? What if something goes wrong? What will people think? What if I fail? What if I look silly? These are the life altering "what if's"; these are the questions that you ask yourself, and at the end of the day when you make the decision you always wonder what would've happened if you would have chosen the other path.

Usually when we jump and make that big decision, if it doesn't work out, we can always look back and know if we had not jumped, where our life would still be. Because you were living that life for a while and it would have just been more of the same.

But it's the saying "no" to that one experience and remaining in that sameness that you always sit and wonder, "what if?" What if we would have taken that leap of faith? What if I would have invested my time into something I was really passionate about? What if I had decided to go ahead and do something that might make me look silly to others?

Those are the no fun "what if's". I'm sure you're just like me, and if you sit and think long enough, there are hundreds of decisions that you made that were good decisions and "what if" decisions. I'm going to share with you a few of the big what-ifs in my life—ones that truly could have changed the direction of my life.

The first one I want to share was one of the first big decisions as a married couple Don and I had to make (next to having children). We had been married several years, and I think our two little girls were around one and three years old. My husband and I had worked really hard to put him through college and then again to get his master's degree.

There were a lot of sacrifices that we made as a couple to put him through school. I give him so much credit because he worked a full-time job and then would drive almost an hour to The Ohio State University to take classes after work.

He would then drive home late in the evening, spend a little time with the girls and I, and turn around and do it all again the next day. He was focused and determined to get his degree, so we did what we had to do to make it happen. He used to tell me how he would get to Columbus 20 minutes early and would try to catch a quick nap or do homework in the car. He was a great example of when you put your mind to something, you do what it takes to make it happen.

Shortly after graduation he was given a job in the offices of the big corporation where he was currently working on the production line. It wasn't too long after that they wanted to interview him for a manager's position at the corporate headquarters in Michigan. Don had already worked at this company for almost 15 years so he had a lot of time in already. This was truly his chance to move up in the company.

He interviewed for the position with the gentleman who was retiring and interviewing people to take his position. He really liked Don and wanted to bring us up to Michigan, have dinner, and talk about the opportunity and what it would look like for us to move there.

I remember Don was so excited about the opportunity. My husband has always been up for anything new and exciting. He loves adventure and he loves doing new things. He even tries to drive different ways to work every day because he's not much on redundancy!

I, on the other hand, am the complete and total opposite. I love structure, I love predictability, and I am not one for change. So let's just say we were going into this trip to Michigan with two totally different visions for how this might look.

When we got there, they put us up in this beautiful condominium overlooking Lake Michigan. The manager and his wife took us out to dinner, and they were such a lovely couple. They really liked us, and he ended up offering the job to my husband.

The next step was for us to come back to look at houses in the area with our girls. This was getting real! The offer had already been made, details had already been discussed, and now it was time to bring the wife up to look at the area and houses to give the okay to move forward. Don had told the gentleman that we needed to do this first before he could give him an answer.

I can remember worrying about a couple of different things. First and foremost, I was worried about leaving my family. I have always been extremely close to my family. My mom, sister, and I actually worked together, and my girls were their only granddaughters. I was so worried about what this might look like.

I remember my husband calling me at work on a Thursday saying that they wanted us to come up on Saturday, and a realtor had houses lined up for us to look at. I was scared to death to tell my mom because I wasn't sure how she was going to take it. I wasn't even sure myself what I wanted to do.

Fear had just set in every vein of my body. I would be giving up the career I had built up for many years as well as the income that came with it.

I remember calling my mom to let her know that I wouldn't be able to work on Saturday because of this last-minute decision that Don's opportunity brought to him. They wanted us to come that day and you most definitely can't say no when it comes to something like this. The reaction that I got from my mom was not a great one. She was not excited about it and didn't try to hide it, but, if I'm being honest, as much as I didn't want my mom to be upset about it, I was a little excited about what this opportunity might look like.

I mean, when your husband graduates from college and starts in corporate America, of course you hope that he gets recognized for his hard work and moves up in the company that he's been with for almost 15 years. That's exactly what was happening.

We went to the little town in Michigan on the lake, and it was such a quaint little town. It had the cutest little downtown area that was right by the lake, and they also had the cutest playground on the beach for the kids. I just remember feeling that hometown feel when we were there.

The realtor took us to many houses over the two days we were there, and the last day, we actually found a house that

I got really excited about. It was the first one we had looked at that I actually was excited about and could see our family living in.

We went back to the condo that night, put the girls to bed, and sat in the living room discussing how this might play out. I remember us both sitting on the couch, and, although I was excited a bit about the opportunity and there was a little piece of me that thought it could be a fun experience, fear was the one that won that night. I remember telling him I just couldn't move. I didn't want to upset my family, I didn't want to leave all of my clients that I had built up over the years, nor did I want to give up that income. I worried how we would get by without it.

I was looking at all the negative and was consumed with all the fear going on in my own head.

When I look back now that I'm much older, I definitely see it in a different way. I remember my husband saying he would support whatever decision I wanted to make, but he wanted me to know that if he turned this job down, he would have to start looking for another job outside of this company where he had been for 15 years. He knew that they would never give him another opportunity after turning down this kind of position.

We made the decision on our way back to Ohio that we were going to stay where we were and that he would start looking for another job at another company. There was a little piece of me that was sad—maybe I did have a little piece of adventurer in me—but for the most part I was happy with the decision we had made: to stay right where we were.

That was the first big decision that we had to make as a married couple that would have totally changed the direction of our lives together. It was also one of the "what-if's" that we often talk about. Where we would be right now had we taken that journey?

There are lots of great things that happened in our lives that would have never happened if we had taken that journey and decided to move our family 4 1/2 hours away from home. I also believe it could have possibly not been a good thing. Maybe it wouldn't have worked; maybe we would have ended up in divorce because we were so unhappy. There are lots of things that could have happened that didn't because we made the decision to stay. But it's the what-ifs from making a decision out of fear that I always wonder how things would have been different.

I often think about how selfish I was to not support my husband with an opportunity of a lifetime. I let my fear of upsetting my family and stepping out of my comfort zone keep me from making a decision for our own little family. Maybe some amazing things would have come from making the decision to go. Maybe our marriage would have gotten stronger. Maybe, maybe, maybe!

Again it's not that I am not grateful for all the amazing things that have happened to us since we made that decision, it's just one of those things where you always look back and wonder "what if".

What if I had been confident enough in myself and in my husband and in our situation to step out in faith and do something out of my realm of comfort? What direction would our lives have taken for the better? I think so many times we let fear step in to our decision-making because we don't have the confidence in ourselves to step out and just jump.

Don ended up getting a job in Columbus, Ohio, which was about a 60-minute drive from home if there was no traffic. But let's be honest, in big cities there is always traffic! He had been driving back and forth for several years working in downtown Columbus, so he was gone a lot. I was still working at the same job in the salon with my family, so my life was still the same.

I would work, take care of my two daughters, my family and friends were around, but it was totally different for my husband. Every day, Don was driving to a different world. He was away from home, away from his daughters, making new friends… needless to say our worlds were going down different paths. At this point in our lives, we found our marriage struggling. Everything that we had known and done in the beginning of our marriage had just changed. We found ourselves at a crossroads. (And I was afraid this would happen if we DID move.)

We could either give up or we could fight to make it work.

It was not an easy time, but we decided that we were going to do everything we could to save our marriage. I remember spending the weekend away together, sitting by the pool at the hotel, making the decision to move closer to his job. We made the decision to move to where we can split the drive to work. I would still work part-time in the salon and he would be closer to his job as well.

We made the decision to move, had our house built, and moved in when I was seven months pregnant for my third child. That was one of those life-changing decisions that you make that even though the change doesn't come easy and it's scary, you have peace about the decision because you know it's what you need to do. I never find myself "what if'ing" that decision.

We moved into our new home, and a few months later, my girls started school, and I gave birth to our third child. We had our cute little family of three. Just a few months after I gave birth, I went back to work part-time.

After the birth of my son, the doctors told me that it was not a good idea for me to have any more children. All of my pregnancies were really rough on me. My body always looked at being pregnant as something foreign invading my body, and it would try its hardest to fight it off like an infection. So, I felt like I had the flu for nine months. I was put in the hospital many times. It really wasn't an easy time for me.

After my son was born, I was told that three was a good number, and if I were to get pregnant again, the outcome could be a lot worse. My body had already been through four pregnancies (I lost my first pregnancy at 4 1/2 months) and a lot of trauma.

About a year later my husband and I were talking and I just told him that I truly felt we were supposed to have another baby. I told him that I really didn't want our younger son growing up without a sibling close in age like his two sisters were. In my spirit I just knew I wasn't done yet, that our family wasn't complete, and I knew he always wanted a big family. We talked about it for a while and came into agreement that I would go to my gynecologist's office and tell my doctor how I felt and if she truly believed that I could withstand another pregnancy.

My doctor had become a friend—I guess when you're in the office as much as I was that's kind of inevitable! But we also shared the same faith. When I went in for my checkup and she asked me how I was doing, I looked at her and said, "I don't know if you're going believe what I'm about ready to say."

She looked at me and said, "Are you wanting to have another baby?" I told her how I was feeling and I asked her if there was physically any reason why I couldn't get pregnant. She told me that physically, there was no reason I couldn't get pregnant, but they were just really worried about what another terrible nine months would do to me especially having three small children.

I told her how I felt and that I really felt deep down in my spirit that we were supposed to have another child. I told her that Don agreed with me, but said that I had to talk to her first and get the green light. I asked her if she would please believe with me for a healthy pregnancy with no complications. I truly believed this time was going to be different.

That day, I left the office with my doctor's total agreement that I was going to get pregnant and have a totally different experience. It wasn't very long after that conversation that I found myself back in the office because I was pregnant for my fourth child. I would love to tell you that I never got sick one day of my pregnancy and it was totally different experience than all the others, but that's not the case.

I started out like I did with all the other pregnancies, I got very sick and struggled every day. I started to let fear come back. I remember lying on the couch one morning trying to muster up enough energy to get dressed when all I really wanted to do was crawl in bed. I was feeling sorry for myself, wondering why I made the decision to do this again, wishing I had a listened to what they told me about not having any more children.

Then all of the sudden, I started coming to the realization that maybe being so sick was teaching me something. Maybe it was so that later in life I would have more sympathy for people that were dealing with illnesses. Maybe it was because someday I would have to deal with something similar to this situation with someone else and I would be able to let them know that I've been there and I understand. Because really in life that's what we look for, is for people to truly understand what we're going through, so we don't feel like we're the only crazy ones out there!

And I have to tell you that as soon as I made that realization, as soon as I accepted it for what it was and stopped fearing it again every morning, I started to feel better. This last pregnancy was the closest thing to what I would call a "normal pregnancy" that I've ever had.

I often laugh and say if I had felt this way through my other pregnancies I would probably have eight children. The last three to four months of that pregnancy were just so easy in comparison to what I had experienced in the past.

This was one of those decisions that there were a lot of what if's, but we decided not to let fear of getting pregnant and how I would feel affect that decision. Fear was never involved in making that decision. We walked in faith on that one, and when we look back on those "what if's" they make us sad. We often say, "what if we would not have had our youngest son?" He has brought so much joy into our lives that we cannot even imagine life without him. We made a decision without fear and without looking back.

We had just had baby number 4, and I was in the process of making the decision of when—and more importantly how—to go back to work! Having young children can be very challenging, especially when parents work. But having four children and no family around to help out was looking to be very challenging. With two young girls in school, a two-year-old, and a brand-new baby, I just started to feel like I should stay home with my children.

Up until now I always had the luxury of working part-time, and while I worked, I had the most amazing women caring for my kids. When I lived near family, my mom would always keep the kids one day a week, and then a dear friend of mine—who is like a grandmother to me and my kids—kept them the other two days. There was nobody better to care of my children than these women in my life.

I never left the house feeling bad about going to work. I'm not going to say that when they were not feeling well that I didn't want to stay home with them, but even if I decided to go to work, I knew that there was nobody better for them to be with than Grandma or Dorothy.

Once we moved away from home, it wasn't quite that easy. I started feeling like I should just stay home with my kids. I didn't have the luxury of calling a family member to swing by and pick up my kids or help me get them to practices. My husband was not in the position at that time where he could run home from work and help either.

So we had to make the decision on me going back to work. Again, this was a really tough decision because I didn't want to disappoint my mom, whom I've worked for almost 20 years. I loved going to work, it was just home to me. My sister and I worked very well together and had so much fun. I loved my career as a stylist and loved my clients!

It is such a great thing when your job is helping make people feel good about themselves. They tell you how great you are, and then they actually pay you for making them feel great! It was a real win-win situation for 20 years. I loved my career and now I was making the decision to step away from it to a much more important career—taking care of my children.

Fear set in again, as I was afraid of upsetting people. I was afraid of upsetting my mom, my clients, and I was nervous about the loss of my income. All of that was based in fear.

I remember finally making the decision to step away from my career and stay home. It was one of those tough decisions in my life that I have never regretted one time. I'm not going to tell you that there weren't times, especially when my kids were young, that I struggled with that decision more for selfish reasons.

I missed dressing up every day, going to work, hanging out with people that I loved, and seeing clients that were more like friends to me. Leaving that world to stay home with four small children really was a huge change for me. That was also a decision that we made that was not easy, but I have never given it a second thought or have that uncomfortable and uneasy "what if" thought.

We tease and say, "if I still worked full time, what a great car I could drive or the fancy purses I could carry! If I had kept working, we could have a bigger house and I could have hired somebody to clean for me." But really it's all just in fun. We made the decision for me to stay home, and although it was not an easy one, it's one that I will never regret doing.

One thing that I knew I was good at and that I had confidence in myself was being a mom. I loved taking care of my kids and running my house. I was confident in that job, so it was an easier decision to make—one I will hold dear for my entire life.

Another huge blessing that came from following my gut and staying home was a year later, my daughter was diagnosed with Juvenile (type 1) Diabetes. That was one of the worst days of my life, but I am so blessed that I was a stay at home mom and could care for her the way I needed to: packing up my 2 little boys in their car seats every day to drive to her school at lunch time to help her give herself a shot; being able to drop everything and run to the school if she needed me.

She was only 9 years old and it was (and still is to this day) a very serious and scary disease. I am so glad my husband and I gave up some things for me to stay home, and I am glad I listened to that inner voice that was telling me it was a good idea.

For 15 years we lived in that house and raised our 4 kids. It was very comfortable. We lived next-door to our best friends and raised our kids together. I often called it my little "Leave It To Beaver" world. Our kids grew up playing outside and playing with other children; it was just a great time.

Don started looking for a new job to try to bring him closer to home. He ended up getting a new position that was literally 10 minutes from our house! We felt this was such a God thing. He often missed the kids sporting events after school because of the long drive from work.

He hated this because he is such an involved dad and never wanted to miss anything with his kids. So when this job opportunity came along, it was just like it was sent down from heaven. We truly thought that this was where he was going to retire from and that he would be there until all the kids were graduated.

Then one day the company decides to restructure, and since Don had only been there about 18 months, he was one of the many people that were let go. We were shocked to say the least, as this had never happened to him before. So the journey of job hunting, resume writing, and interviewing started again.

He had an amazing opportunity with a company, that we soon discovered meant him working in another city that was about an hour and twenty minutes away from our home. But when you're in a position where you have four children and no job, you need to look at all opportunities that are presented to you.

So he decided to take the job. The company offered to relocate us to the new area, to which, again, I was not a fan of doing. I was content, comfortable, and in my world of sameness, and the thought of uprooting our family and moving scared me to death. You would think that since I often wondered "what if" from the last move opportunity that I would have been a little quicker to jump this time—a little more excited maybe to take a new journey. But that was not the case at all. Once again, I used every excuse why it was not a good idea.

One daughter was in college and had made the decision to go to that specific college because it was close to home. Our other daughter was getting ready to graduate from college, so what would she do? Our boys were in the middle of their junior high years—what a terrible time to move. I could name every excuse for why we should not do this.

So for several months my husband would drive back and forth to work. I knew this was not the best situation but fear had overtaken me again and I just couldn't do it. What's funny is I remember talking to my kids all separately about it and every single one of them was all for it! I guess they have more of their dad in them when it comes to adventure than they do their mom and her comfort zone living. And I'm so grateful for that!

It was actually the conversation that I had with my then 13-year-old son that really hit me. He was saying "let's do it mom, let's get the heck out of here!" that made me realize, if he can do it, then so can I.

A few weeks later at a baseball tournament, my husband and I took a walk around the park between games and had a heart-to-heart conversation about what relocating might look like. We talked about how we wanted our kids to know that it's okay to do things that are scary and know that it's okay to take adventures and to try new things. If it doesn't work out, you can always go back. We stood there on this trail at the park in Indiana and made the decision this time that we were going to go. I was so scared but so excited at the same time. We hugged and I cried, nervous tears of joy and sadness.

Now I'd like to say that from there on out the journey was fun and I was excited and we moved and it was easy and great. It wasn't that easy.

Trying to sell a house, find a new house, having your children change their position on wanting to leave—all not fun.

My two sons decided once school started back from the summer break and they were back with old friends, that leaving wasn't the best idea and they weren't a fan of it at all. So the energy in the house had shifted, as the excitement of looking for houses and the move all changed. There was no looking back now.

FEAR: Stories We Tell Ourselves

We sold our house right around the holidays and the stress of finding a house around the holidays was not a fun one. I remember when I told my than 13-year-old son we finally sold our house, he broke down in tears. I had not seen him cry like that in years, and it just broke my heart. My stress level was at an all-time high! What had we done?

Several weeks later the moving truck came, packed up all of our stuff and moved us to this new town where we knew absolutely no one. I can tell you that this probably was one of the most challenging, but one of the most rewarding and fun things we have ever done.

What I learned from this process and this whole experience was that sometimes change is good! Sometimes we need to get out of our comfort zones to experience life in a different way. Sometimes we are so set in our ways and our traditions, the way things have to be, that we are not open to experience new things and new journeys and new people. I believe that a lot of our decisions are based out of fear and the lack of confidence that we have in ourselves.

My boys decided they weren't ready to move because they weren't confident in themselves enough to know that they were going to walk into a school and make new friends and be just fine. They got in their own heads telling themselves that this was going to be terrible. Nobody was going to know who they were, and they were not going to know anybody. They weren't going to fit in. They were leaving the only world they had ever known their entire life, and it was scary.

If I'm being honest, there is no way I would have wanted to have moved when I was their age. Heck, I didn't want to move when I was a grown adult for the same fears that they were having as middle schoolers.

People often do not recognize the impact fear has in their lives, simply because they use different words to describe the emotion—words such as worry, nervousness, stress, shyness, or anxiety. I know that it was for me. I would not think I was fearful of something, just extremely stressed by it or nervous about how it would turn out.

But the biggest fear I think most of us deal with is the fear of failure. Fear of failure is what restricts me to my comfort zone. It is what makes me avoid risks and play it safe as the years pass by.

Can you relate to any of my stories?

Did you ever make decisions in your life that you just knew were the right ones, even when the decision was not always a favorable or popular one?

Have you made those decisions that you look back on now and then and wonder "what if"?

Has fear or lack of confidence played a role in any of those decisions?

Since this journey I have learned to take on a totally new mindset.

Your Crowning Moment

If You Can't Beat Fear,
Do it Scared.
—Glennon Doyle Melton

Great Quotes

"The fears we don't face become our limits."
—Robin Sharma

"Fear kills more dreams than failure ever will."
—Unknown

"Everything we ever wanted is on the other side of fear."
—George Addair

"F-E-A-R has 2 meanings. Forget Everything And Run or Face Everything And Rise. The Choice is Yours."
—Zig Ziglar

"Fear doesn't exist anywhere except the mind."
—Unknown

Fear is often what holds you back from your success, living life to its fullest and new experiences. You are scared of taking chances because you fear losing the security and comfort that you have now. Even if you aren't content you try to convince yourself that you are happy in your current state when in fact, you are not. Your self-talk may sound positive in your attempt to lie to yourself. But somehow, there is an inner knowing that you are short changing yourself.

Ask yourself what you are afraid of. What is the worst thing that can happen? Take a step-by-step approach in breaking down your fears and see if there is any way too look at things more positively. When you confront your fears, you will often realize that the worst case scenario is not as bad as you think.

In fact, the benefits of change are worth the risk. Sometimes change is just what the doctor ordered.

I told you about my husband's new job and how we decided to move to another city, put our boys in a new school, and begin life in an area we had never even been before nor knew anybody. It was a huge change for not only myself but my whole family.

My husband loves change and was so excited for a new adventure. For me, I feared it something terrible! I came up with, once again, all the reasons why it was not a good idea to move. I started to think about all the wrong, negative reasons why it was not a good idea. After a while of living in that negative space, I checked myself and reminded myself that I did not want to look back and wonder "what if" this time. I wanted to try to embrace change and do something different, after 15 years of living in the same place. I could come up with the hundred and one reasons why we should stay and my mind was only giving me a few reasons why we should go. But I started to realize that my fear was holding me back and it was the fear of the unknown that didn't want me to try this change.

Change can be good. It can be a very positive thing, even if it is something you may fear a bit.

I can't tell you that once we made the decision to move that everything went smoothly and there were no bumps in the road. No, that's not the way it went, and honestly, that's not the way life works. But I will say that even during the trying times, keeping a positive attitude and outlook and doing a lot of positive self-talk, you will get to the other side. That's life in general; no matter what's going on, we all need to continue to try to see the positives in all situations.

What I can tell you is that from this big change it has been such a growing experience and something that I'm sure will be up in my top of my life changing experiences.

Moving somewhere that I didn't know anyone challenged me to get out of my comfort zone and get out and meet new people. And I truly love meeting people.

It reminded me how much I love decorating and making a house a home. It was so exciting to have something new again. Yard work was once again enjoyable because it was also new. And let's get this straight, I do **not** like yard work one bit! But the first year, it was kind of fun going outside and discovering new blooming flowers, bushes, and what all is on our property. Oh, and decorating for the holidays has been exciting again. All the things that had gotten so mundane after 15 years in the same house was taking on new meaning again, kind of how Christmas takes on a new direction when you have your first child.

I was going on walks and walking to places I had never been before. I felt like I was on vacation but it was a very lengthy vacation. Christmas time was a little more exciting. When you're used to seeing the same Christmas lights at the same places and then you move somewhere new, just driving to the grocery store in the evening is exciting because you're seeing all these new Christmas decorations that you've never seen before. I could go on and on about all the little things that I had no idea to even put on my list of positives when I was deciding if this was something I could do.

Obviously there are many other things we face every day that can require change, not all things are life changing events. We can still get caught up in fear. It's not easy to let go of fear, especially when it is the fear of the unknown. Our minds tell us that what we do know is much safer. That's just human nature and your imagination will come up with dozens of reasons to fear the unknown. Once you understand this, it is easier to understand why you are coming up with all these excuses and then do your best to rationalize them, process the real outcome, and let the negative thoughts go. If you are playing the "what if" game, then you know it is usually coming from a place of fear. Why do we spend so much energy imagining the worst when there is just as much chance that the outcome will be amazing?

Socrates once said, "The secret of change is to focus all of your energy, not on fighting the old, but on building the new." **Making a big change is scary, but regret is even scarier.** It's all the little blessings that come when you decide to get out of your comfort zone and do something different. Make a change. Change is good and we shouldn't fear it. The key to change is just to let go of all that fear. Change could be leading you to a new beginning.

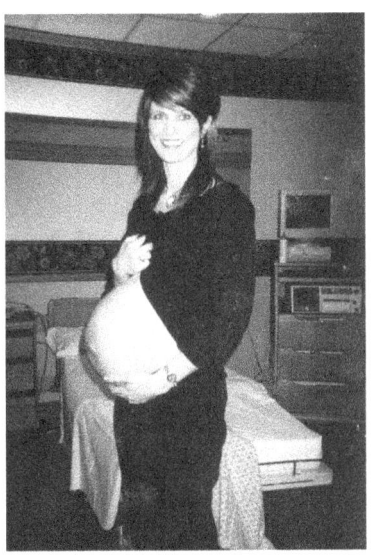

Ready to deliver 9lb.9oz. baby #3

After fearing I would never get my body back,
I worked hard to prove I could do it.

Staying home to raise these 4 amazing children

Looking through the rear view mirror as we pull away from our home of 15 years into a new adventure.

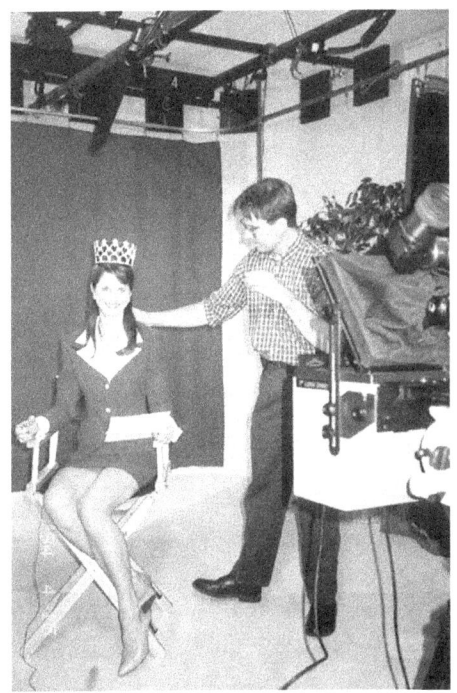

Filming a commercial

Grand Marshall at many parades

MISS CONCEPTION #4

It's Too Late

Do you remember being a kid and someone asking you what you wanted to be when you grew up? How about sitting in your bedroom with your best friend talking and planning out your wedding before you were even old enough to have a boyfriend. You planned out the color scheme and who you wanted to be your bridesmaids. It is so fun to think about our lives when we are young. The opportunities are endless!

We do some great dreaming at that age. And it doesn't start as a teenager. Ask any six-year-old what they want to be when they grow up, and you'll get all kinds of great answers. They'll tell you exactly what they want to be with such animation and excitement in their voices.

Talk to a college student about their dreams and aspirations and you'll get all kinds of answers. Some won't know what they want to do, but they know that the whole world is open to them. Others will have an exact plan of what's going to happen with their lives. It all comes down to dreaming and dreaming big.

Then we get to be young adults and we start talking about our boyfriends and getting married, or maybe we are married, and we start talking about having children and how many we want. We think about where we want to live and maybe moving up the corporate ladder or starting our own business. Again, so much dreaming and goal setting at such a great time in life.

When my husband and I first started dating we would always sit down and write out our five-year plan with our goals. Then we would put it in an envelope and seal it up and tuck it away in a drawer somewhere with the date stamped on it to open—kind of like a time capsule.

We would open it up five years later and circled the ones that came true and the ones that we missed. We did that for about the first fifteen years we were together, during the time where we were dreaming and in the middle of our lives and our jobs and our children. We were so busy dreaming and building our lives with such great expectancy.

Years go by, some dreams we made and met, others fell short. There were always new, unexpected twists and turns along the way, but it was all part of living our lives in a busy, busy world. Dreaming and setting goals is such a huge part of our lives, then one day we find ourselves just living in the day-to-day routine. We get so caught up in our lives and everything that's going on until one day, we're sitting wondering where the time went.

I've always been a dreamer, very entrepreneurial in my spirit, an idea person. When I set a goal, I love working hard to achieve it. Then came a time when I just felt "blank". That's just the best word that I can use to describe it.

When I was younger I had a career in the fashion industry, and it kind of defined who I was. I loved being trendy, I loved educating and training stylists, and I loved talking every day with my clients. I was also a mom of four young children that kept me extremely busy. I was also the mom of a child with a disease that I had to help manage and control. I became an advocate and educator for diabetes and a health and wellness coach.

Then my oldest daughter went to college, and my second daughter followed behind two years later. My boys were getting older and didn't need me in the same capacity that they did when they were little. It was starting to hit me how quickly time passes. My oldest son will be going to college in a few years followed two years later by my youngest son. I felt "blank'.

When I would think about it, I would get so sad imagining that this part of my life is almost over. The hustle and bustle of being a mom, feeling the high stress times that you wished away because you're exhausted, all the changing of diapers and healing scraped knees, counseling through a broken heart from a break up, the disappointment of not being allowed to go to a party where all the cool kids will be, it would all be over. Going through the motions of everything motherhood brings when all of the sudden you see it slowly coming to an end, you would give anything to get it back and start all over again.

I came to a point in my life where I just felt blank. I talk to women all the time that feel the exact same way: women whose children are all moved out and are grown adults with families of their own, women who just feel lost without a real sense of purpose anymore, no goals to move towards. Some even just feel like the best part of their lives are over. I can say I had some of these same feelings when I hit my 50s, and **I still had 2 young teenage boys at home!** This is what really hit me—if I was feeling this way now, how was I going to feel in a few years when they are both out of the house and living their lives full of endless dreams and possibilities.

You see, I had packed so much of my worth into my accomplishments and how I looked, but now that I'm older and not a youthful 25-year-old anymore, I had to sit down and really evaluate how I saw this next chapter of my life.

I'm not going to lie; I did get in a place of comfort. We had a nice house, the kids were all doing great, and it was very routine—the way I have a tendency to like it. But I had lost that fire, that excitement of trying something new, of pushing myself to achieve a goal. I realized when I started digging deep that it was because I just felt like that part of my life was over. Kind of crazy right? I work with women all of the time, helping them with personal development. A lot of time is spent mapping out a strategy for where they want to go and how to get there. I found myself being able to give great advice to other people but came to a place where I needed to implement that same process into my own life.

An opportunity for me to become a state director for a Mrs. pageant and to work more with coaching girls who were in the pageant world presented itself to me. This was a great fit for me because I love what pageants can do for women. I know a lot of times that the pageant world gets a really bad rap. I think that there are always the extremes to where those stereotypes happen, but for me, pageantry helped mold me into the woman I am today.

My journey in pageantry taught me a lot of the essential things that I needed for what I love to do to this day. If you would have asked me at the age of 20 if I saw myself speaking in front of large groups, holding seminars for organizations, becoming a national spokesperson for a huge organization, speaking to doctors from all over the world, and now writing a book, I would have laughed and told you there was no possible way I would do any of that stuff.

I had no self-esteem or confidence in my early twenties to even begin to think in that direction. And although I talk about how I still had low self-esteem during my time at the Miss USA pageant, I have certainly come a long way from where I was before that time.

As I grew and continued in that journey I learned so much more about myself and gained confidence. I ended up finding out that I absolutely love motivating, inspiring, and giving talks to groups of 10 to 10,000 people. So when I had the opportunity to become a director, I was so excited to be able to help women grow into their full potential and achieve a goal that they had set for themselves.

Since my daughters were no longer at home and my boys were at an age where they were in school or doing sports, I had a little more time to start coaching girls that were interested in pageantry as well.

I had more time to focus on what I was possibly going to do in this chapter of my life. I thought being a director was it. But after two years of directing, I was asked to be on the national staff of the International pageant system. It was a great honor and an opportunity that I was excited to take.

It's Too Late

My circle of influence became much bigger as I was going to now be able to help women from all over the world achieve their goals.

Then it hit me—I realized that my love for helping women grow and achieve amazing things was keeping me from working on my own dreams and goals. I was helping women become the best version of themselves, but I had not fulfilled a dream that had been seeded in me for many years.

My dream for many years was envisioning myself standing on the stage in front of thousands and thousands of people, speaking and inspiring women. I remember having my first experience of what I wanted to do when I was probably 21 years old at a huge cosmetology convention in Chicago. It was my first big beauty show, and I was so excited to be there.

My mom is a stylist and had gone every year with her staff to this huge event in Chicago, and I had heard all the great things about being there. I was so excited to go for my first time. For those of you that have no idea what an international beauty show is like, it's a huge event held in a convention center, full of products, vendors, and stages teaching you about new things in the industry. Then there are all these extra classes that you sign up for that are held in their own rooms. There are special haircutting techniques or skincare classes, and there are also motivational classes where you sit and listen to someone who inspires you to be a better person and a better stylist.

Of all the amazing things that were there, I remember sitting in on an inspirational Michael Cole class. I remember sitting in that class just in awe of how on earth somebody can talk for an hour and teach and motivate. It was just the coolest thing ever, and it made me feel so powerful, so alive, so ready to conquer the world. There was just something about that class that I loved.

Now at that time I never thought that I would want to do that kind of thing, but I knew that there was something special about it because it had the power to motivate and help people.

My first vision of myself being a speaker was at a *Women of Faith Conference* many years ago. I had to be in my early 30's when I went for the first time, and those women were inspiring. They were at a completely different level than I have ever experienced. To see thousands and thousands of women totally enjoying being there together and supporting each other, totally engrossed in every word that the speakers were talking about, was an amazing experience. Just thinking of the impact that those speakers had on their audience was all inspiring to me. I know that I left there a different person because of what they planted in me during that conference.

One seed that was planted in me that weekend was this vision of someday doing the same thing. That someday I would be sharing my message to thousands of people and planting sends of greatness within them. That has been a vision that I've held onto for many, many years but never really acted upon it in the magnitude that I envisioned it.

I mean I'm a speaker, educator, and a trainer and I work with people one-on-one, in small groups, and in seminars. I've spoken to groups of 500 or more about different topics. I've even been on stage in front of a group of 10,000 people, but it wasn't in the capacity of my vision. I wasn't doing what I wanted to do which was to inspire, uplift, motivate, and give love and encouragement to people. So I've always held on to that little seed, that vision, that dream that's always been deep inside of me.

Then one day I decided I needed to start implementing what I teach to others to myself. I started realizing that I wanted to make this chapter in my life something amazing, something big! It didn't matter that I was now in my 50s, the best part of my life was **not** over.

I started being grateful that the wonderful things in my life **had** happened and stopped being sad that they were over. I started to dream again! I started to make plans for myself. I started to tell myself that I'm never too old to do wonderful things. No matter how big or how small it may seem to you, the only important thing is that you do something.

(Matthew 17:20 "Because of your little faith. Truly I tell you, if you have faith as small as a mustard seed, you can say to this mountain, 'Move from here to there,' and it will move. Nothing will be impossible for you.")

Several years ago I remember working with a friend who had just stopped dreaming. She said what so many women say and feel, that she felt stuck in life, work, and in the same old things. We talked about her passion and dreams and what she had always wanted to do. Throughout this discussion, she told me that she had always wanted to take a class with her Border Collie in agility training. She said that she always thought that would be so fun and something she's always wanted to do but she just never took the time to do it.

The challenge was put out there for her to start the process and look into where she may be able to take that first step and take a class with her dog. It wasn't too much longer after that and she was in her first agility training class with her dog. It was a huge step for her, but I can tell you it was life-changing.

It's probably been 10 years ago that she started that first class, but she took that first step, and today I'm always seeing her Facebook post of the many awards that her now three dogs have won, all the amazing places that she's traveling, and all the fabulous people that she's met along the way. This was a dream of hers, that she never acted upon because she didn't think she had the time, money, or energy to do it. It's a great example of someone implementing a plan and finding joy in the journey.

I have another client that was feeling empty. She was in a place in her life where her kids were grown, and she was not fulfilled anymore in her work. She just accepted it as the way things are when you get to this time of your life. She lived her life so stressed out and unfulfilled and feeling like her best years were behind her. She had stopped dreaming, stopped reaching for more out of life.

Working through her passions and what she loves and has always wanted to do, she decided to go out on her own and start her own boutique. Now she is excited every day with all the new adventures and challenges that come with living her life with purpose.

Everybody's dream is different: to some, your dream may seem small, to others, your dream may feel way too big. What matters most is what that dream looks like to you.

Maybe you've always dreamed of having a cooking class but never really knew how to do it. Maybe you just need to start holding a class, having friends over, advertising, and seeing where it grows and where it goes from there. Perhaps it's starting a book club in your home but having visions of it growing into a once-a-month, huge event. Who knows what it looks like for you, but you need to find something.

If we have no desires, no excitement, nothing to look forward to, nothing to push towards, we go inward, get depressed and our lives just can be unbearable. They feel "blank".

I decided that I was going to push for my own dream. I realized that my age doesn't matter, my looks don't matter, my weight and body image do not matter. All that matters with my dream is that I work really hard to be transparent about my life so that I may help others.

Your Crowning Moment

Let's Dream Again

"Dreams are renewable. No matter what our age or condition, there are still untapped possibilities within us and new beauty waiting to be born."
—Dr. Dale E. Turner

Step 1: *"If you can imagine it, you can achieve it. If you can dream it, you can become it."* —William Arthur Ward

Give yourself permission to dream and be willing to see your live in a new way. Spend time really thinking about what it is that you always dreamed of doing. Start making a list and don't hold back! Don't second-guess yourself by saying "well that's not achievable," or "that's too big and would never happen". Just be all in and write a list of things that you've always wanted to do or to achieve—that thing you always thought you would be doing with your life.

A really great place to start is to ask yourself what you are passionate about. What do you love doing and you would do it even if nobody paid you a penny to do it? What are some of the fun things that you really enjoy doing?

Maybe you love painting, or have a knack at organizational things. Maybe you love training pets, reading, running a marathon, fitness competitions, fashion, writing, or decorating. I could sit and go on and on with a list of things. This is going to be something that you'll have to do specifically for you. No right or wrong answers, don't overthink it, just make your list.

Step 2: *"The indispensable first step to getting the things you want out of life is this: decide what you want."* —Ben Stein

Now pick! Pick where you want to start, pick that thing that just makes you excited at this very moment. Something that you have always wanted to do. I told you the story about my friend who had always wanted to take a dog agility class with her dog. At the time it seemed like something she thought about but she would never do it. She thought it was a silly goal. But it was really on her heart as something she had always dreamed of but never thought of actually acting on that dream. It meant enough to her that she wrote that down and that was her goal.

Find what it is that you want and write it down. I always tell people to write it down on three or four notecards and then post those notes cards in places that you will see them every day. Maybe on the dash of your car or your mirror in the bathroom. Maybe on the bottom of your computer screen. Keep it in front of you so you know what it is that you're working towards with your new dream.

Step 3: ***"The future belongs to those who believe in the beauty of their dreams."*** —Eleanor Roosevelt

I have always been motivated by quotes. I will grab ahold of one and write it down and post it everywhere I can see it to get that message deep inside me! It goes back to my believe in self-talk. What we feed our spirit is as important as what we feed our body.

I am going to share with you several great quotes about dreaming and goal setting. Grab ahold of the one or two that speak to you and inspire you to move forward in your journey to a new adventure. Or find your own that you love. Write them down on that same note card right under your dream or goal. Keep those cards visible where you see them all the time.

"Go confidently in the direction of your dreams. Live the life you've imagined."
—Henry David Thoreau

"When you have a dream you've got to grab it and never let go."
—Carol Burnett

"What's the purpose of living if you don't go after your dreams?"
—Samson Reiny

"I can do all things through Christ who strengthens me."
Philippians 4:13

It's Too Late

"You are never too old to set another goal or to dream a new dream."
—C.S. Lewis

"Twenty years from now you will be more disappointed by the things you didn't do than by the ones you did. So throw off the bowlines. Sail away from the safe harbor. Catch the trade winds in your sails. Explore. Dream. Discover."
—Mark Twain

"Capture your dreams and your life becomes full. You can, because you think you can."
—Nikita Koloff

"To accomplish great things, we must not only act, but also dream; not only plan, but also believe."
—Anatole France

"For those who dare to dream, there is a whole world to win."
—Dhirubhai Ambani

"Not fulfilling your dreams will be a loss to the world, because the world needs everyone's gift—yours and mine."
—Barbara Sher

"Keep your heart open to dreams. For as long as there's a dream, there is hope, and as long as there is hope, there is joy in living."
—Anonymous

"Any dream worth dreaming, is worth the effort to make it come true."
—Evan Gourley

"Go for it now. The future is promised to no one."
—Wayne W. Dyer

"At first, dreams seem impossible, then improbable, and eventually inevitable."
—Christopher Reeve

"This one step: choosing a goal and sticking to it, changes everything."
—Scott Reed

"It's better to have an impossible dream than no dream at all."
—Anonymous

"Be willing to be uncomfortable. Be comfortable being uncomfortable. It may get tough, but it's a small price to pay for living a dream."
—Peter McWilliams

Step 4: *"Start researching that dream and let the journey begin."* —Lisa Moser

I love the quote in step one by William Ward that says, *"If you can imagine it, you can achieve it, if you can dream, it you can become it".*

Lots of motivational speakers and things you will read will tell you the part about just dreaming big and imagine it will happen—manifesting what you want out of life.

The part that they sometimes leave out is that you have to be actively pursuing that dream. You can't just sit in your living room and dream about it and do nothing to make it happen. That's a part of the journey, and honestly, an exciting part of the journey. I always try to tell my kids it's not necessarily the destination but the journey where you find the most joy. The things that you learn along the way, the successes and setbacks, they are all a part of your journey to reach your dreams.

So my advice to people who have set their mind on something is to do what we talked about in the previous steps and then you have to start putting in the work. You have to start researching your dream. Whatever it is that you decided to do you have to figure out the steps to take to get there. Sometimes you may need to find a mentor, someone that has done what you inspired to do.

Let's say that your goal is to do a fitness competition. You have always dreamed of being it top notch shape and competing in a fitness competition. BUT you don't eat healthy and you don't work out. If you were to just jump in and start going outside and walking every day and thinking "oh, I'll add fruit to my diet because that's healthy", and then after a couple of months you didn't see any real transformation happening, you didn't see your body changing much or feeling any better about things, then you're going to get discouraged and probably tell yourself that that is why you never pursued that dream in the first place—because it really was a silly goal for you.

But if you approach this goal, this dream of yours, in a different way, you will most likely have much better success. Maybe you start getting on the Internet and googling fitness competitors. Maybe you join a gym and find a personal trainer or find a friend that knows about the fitness world.

Then you start learning what you need to do to train for a fitness competition—how you have to change your diet and learn about the different muscles and different exercises. Then maybe the next step, once you're seeing results, is learning how competitions work—what different competitions there are and maybe set your sights on one to start with. Then set up a calendar of steps to take to get to that point.

Whatever your dream is you have to do your homework. Take it step-by-step so you don't get too overwhelmed. Be excited about what you're doing. Share with people what you're doing. You will know that you're doing something you love because you will be so excited with each new step that you make. And even when you have a setback, it won't rattle you too badly because you are so excited that you are working towards your dream to do something new.

When I am working towards something, for instance writing this book, there was a lot of research that went in for me to figure this all out. Then I had to find a mentor, someone that could help me do this—someone that has been there, done that, and can help walk me through the process to keep some of the mistakes minimal.

Reaching this goal has been challenging. There were days that I just really didn't know what the heck I was doing. I wondered what I got myself into. There was some self-doubt coming in, but when that would happen I would quickly read my cards and know what I was working towards. I would remember that finishing the book was going to be the beginning of the new exciting journey for me. The beginning of that little seed and dream that was planted in me many, many years ago.

I am writing this book in hopes that I can reach thousands and thousands of people to inspire, uplift, encourage and motivate. To help them know they are not alone and that everyone deals with *stuff*. To help them understand that the grass is not greener in someone else's yard and that every single yard has weeds in it somewhere. To stop comparing ourselves to others and to live our best life and to find joy in every day. My dream and my aspirations are to speak life into people, to put a fire under someone to do something they have never done before. And that is what I wish for you!

Young and dreaming about our future

Our family singing on stage in a Christmas production.

At the Mrs. International pageant

Setting goals and winning a top award in my business

On stage at Mrs. International

Official Mrs. International headshot

MISS CONCEPTION #5

Being Healthy Means Eating Salads

The World Health Organization defines health as a state of complete physical, mental and social well-being, and not merely the absence of disease or infirmity.

Being healthy means so much more than eating salads and getting exercise every day. For most people, when they think of the word "healthy" they automatically think it is time for a strict diet and a high-intensity exercise program to lose excess weight. But it means so much more. There are so many different aspects to the word healthy, and for me, being a healthy person is all about balance in every aspect of my life.

There are many aspects to living a healthy, well balanced life. I like to break it down into eight very important segments in a pie graph. **Spirituality, physical health, family, personal development, self-image, career and finances, friends and social life, and technology.**

The key to living a healthy life is trying to make sure all of these areas are well-balanced. It is like juggling and making sure none of the balls are dropped. The only problem is we tend to let the balls fall that don't seem as important to us or may be a little more challenging to keep in the air.

There have been many times in my life that one or more of these areas were extremely out of balance, and when they were, I could really feel the effects. In doing some research for this section of the book I came across a talk that I had done at church several years ago when all four of my kids were very young. I want to share this story because I think so many people, no matter what your age, will be able to relate to this story in some way. Go ahead and insert your own struggles and stresses.

Monday started off like every Monday: kids to get ready for school, lunches to pack, business partners that needed my help, and the proverbial weekly list of things that needed to be done. I was off to the races that week like most weeks, then Tuesday came. I was asked to give a 45-minute motivational talk to a large group of teens and was happy to say yes! I love doing that kind of thing, although for this group of young women I didn't have a specific talk or something I had previously used, so I knew it would require some work and time on my part—No big deal.

Some of the things that were on my list of duties already for the week were like every mother—laundry, dishes, cooking, housework (those are daily things, not weekly), plus a preschool trip, a first grade trip, three costumes to finish up for Halloween, candy bags to get ready for church Wednesday night, trick-or-treat candy bags for our neighborhood, my son's seventh birthday party at our house, plus appointments spread in through the week with clients. No big deal—or was it?

*Wednesday I found myself leaving for my first-grade son's field trip that was 30 minutes **south** of my house with my four-year-old in tow, ready to help with all the kids in his first-grade class. He was so excited that morning when he left for school that I was coming to the pumpkin farm to see him.*

*As I was following my directions out to the middle of nowhere, there in the road in front of me was a "road closed" sign with no detour to follow. I had no idea where I was nor did I have any other directions to follow, just the direct route to get where I was going. Just as I was about to call my husband to MapQuest it for me to get me around it, my 12-year-old daughter calls me. She tells me her insulin pump is beeping, she is out of insulin, and she needs me to bring all of her supplies to school so she can replace it. Her school is 20 minutes **north** of our house! In that moment, I had an extreme sense of being very overwhelmed.*

I have been driving to the field trip with a hundred things on my mind of what I needed to do when I got home. Now I found myself trying to figure out how to be two places at once, two kids needed me at the very same time. Do I continue onto the field trip (if I can even find it) and tell my daughter that she would just have to skip her lunch and wait until she gets home from school to eat? Or do I disappoint my son by not showing up to his field trip? I truly just wanted to pull over and cry but I knew my son in the backseat would not understand my little breakdown. Or maybe he would, he has them quite often but it's usually because his brother won't play with him or some other life altering event.

I called my husband, we talked about the situation, and I eventually found the pumpkin farm. My daughter came home hungry, but she survived and it all worked out—at least for that half of the day. I pushed through the next two days more stressed than ever. So many things to get done and people to help. Oh, and I did forget to mention the 10 dozen cookies I promised to bake for a friend by Saturday for the prison ministry she is a part of.

I found myself in a place that I teach people not to go. I do talks about living a balanced life for crying out loud! If I get overwhelmed it is usually very short-lived, as I can usually pull myself right out of it. This seemed to be lasting a whole week with no end in sight.

Friday morning the stress level was reaching an all-time high as I drove to my son's school for the fall party they were having in class that afternoon when my phone rings. I was informed that my dad was on his way to the hospital by ambulance. He just had a stroke. I finally reached an all-time high for the week. I felt like I was sinking into a hole and couldn't climb out. I needed to talk this out with someone who understood completely.

I called my dear friend Rochelle who is also a mom of four children and I unloaded all my frustrations. She listened with her amazing, understanding heart and then reminded me of what she and I always talk about. There is no way we can do everything we need to do, and do it well, by ourselves. We need God to help us every day to give us the strength, patience, and guidance in everything we do. We need to express gratitude every morning for what we have and ask God to help us with our day. Let Him know we just cannot do it by ourselves and we need Him to help us.

I always tell people God is the best business partner you could ever have, and I needed my friend to give me a little reminder. Sometimes we get so busy that our prayer life seems to take a backseat.

She and I talked about being a light in people's lives and the only way to do that is to walk with God and let His light shine *through us. How that was the best gift we can give anyone? I was so thankful for our talk and I went on to press through my day.*

So now it's Sunday evening and the end of the week and I have remembered to ask God to walk with me every morning since our talk. I know that it won't be the last time I feel stressed or need a friend to remind me of what I always preach to others. My dad is home and doing fantastic and everything got done that needed to be done for that week. I just remember why I need God with me, because I can't do everything by myself.

And the best part of this story is that a friend stopped by a few days later and just wanted to tell me about a sermon she heard. She said that the pastor was talking about how people have a light that shines in them and others are drawn to them because of that light. He spoke of how the light can be inspirational and a great sense of strength to others. She said she just wanted to stop by to let me to know that she drew inspiration and strength from my light.

Thanks God! I read you loud and clear.

Have you had days, weeks, or even months like this? It's funny how it can seem all consuming when it is happening, but when I found this talk I had given I had totally forgotten about it. We put so much time and energy and focus on things when they're going wrong. When we feel overwhelmed and think we are never going to make it through. We can spend so much time in that negative space and then it just seems to bring on more negativity.

Have you ever met people that are just constantly living in that negative, victim mentality? They always say how everything always goes wrong for them. They'll use phrases like "of course this happened to me," or "I can never catch a break," or "if it's gonna happen to somebody, it's gonna happen to me," or "I have the worst luck."

It's easy to live in that mind set because at times we get so overwhelmed by things that are happening. The one thing that I've learned is if I start to feel like I'm going down that road, I need to talk it out with someone that I know understands and that can help give me a better perspective.

What you don't want to do is talk to someone that is in your same negative, overwhelmed mind frame. The worst thing I could have done that day was to call a friend that I knew would roll around in the muck with me. I always tell people you need to *call up*! Call someone who is a step up from where you want to be in this particular moment. Someone that you know will understand but help give you perspective and some positivity.

Then *look up* and pray! I also know that when I get in a negative head space that my prayer life is probably not where it should be.

Usually I've lost my sense of gratitude and I'm focusing only on myself and my issues and stress.

There are many, many other stories that I could share with you, times where my life has gotten out of balance. You have read about many of the stories in the previous sections of this book. I talk about my quest for trying to earn everybody's love and find my worth and the struggles that came from all my focus being there. I was way out of whack with the health piece when I was struggling with my body image. So many other things in my life were struggling and not in balance at all because all of my focus was on this one thing. And giving up my career to stay home was a big hit to the career and finance pieces.

I believe you can relate to this. Wouldn't you love to learn how to get a little more balance into your life? Let's move right to the "Crowning Moment" on this section. I think this is so relatable for everyone that I don't need to share a bunch of my stories of unbalance—and trust me I have a million and will always be working on this one.

Your Crowning Moment

The More Balanced Your Life, The More Joy You Feel!

Health and Wellness Wheel

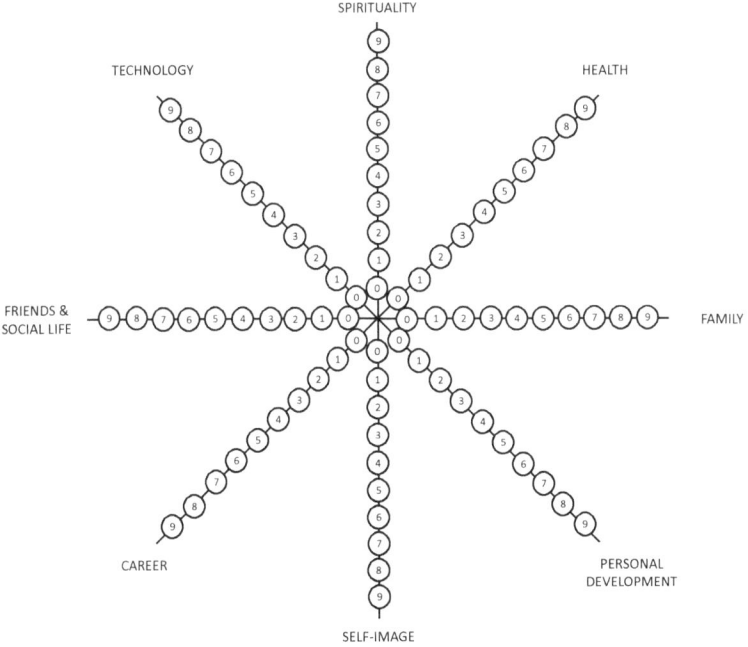

To download the wheel go to: www.LisaMoser.com/wheel

On the chart, rate your area of satisfaction on a scale of 0-9 and mark it on the graph. Zero being not satisfied at all in that area of your life to nine being you feel 100% fulfilled and happy with where you are with that area of your life. Now connect the dots from one to the next to form some sort of outer circle.

Spirituality - How connected are you with your spiritual beliefs. Do you feel satisfied with the time and energy that you give this part of your life?

Physical Health - How physically healthy are you? Do you have the energy and stamina you desire? Are you happy with your level of fitness and activity you do? Are you satisfied with your current eating habits and weight?

Family - Do you feel a close connection to your family? Are your relationships healthy and supportive? Do you spend quality time with the ones you love?

Personal Development - How invested are you with some form of personal development? Do you try to grow and push yourself to be your best? Do you try to learn new things and experience passion with goal setting? Are you constantly working to become the best version of yourself?

Self-Image - Do you respect and love yourself unconditionally? Do you practice positive self-talk? How highly do you think of your abilities? Do you build yourself up?

Career and Finances - Do you enjoy your career? Are you headed towards the direction you want to go with it? Are you exploring new possibilities? Are you satisfied with your current finances?

Friends and Social Life - Are you surrounding yourself with positive supportive people? Do your friends encourage you and bring positivity to your life? Are you having fun in your life and getting out to experience new things?

Technology - Do you currently have a healthy balance when it comes to social media and technology? Do you not let your life get hacked by cell phones, Facebook, Instagram, television and the wonderful world of "virtual reality"? Do you have a good sense of balance when it comes to spending time with technology and spending time in the real world?

Being Healthy Means Eating Salads

Now connect your dots. How does your wheel look? Is it well balanced or do you see flat areas in your circle? Take a minute and just really study it, are you surprised at any of the areas?

For those areas you score 7-9, congratulations you are very satisfied in those areas and it's important for you to maintain what you're doing to keep yourself satisfied. BUT don't overlook that there may be areas for improvement and that you are not limiting your potential to further grow in that area.

If you scored a 4-6 in any of the categories, then I would say you're probably pretty satisfied but definitely have room to grow and explore. Think about how and what you may do to grow a bit in that area.

If your score is a 3 or below in a certain category, then that is an area you may really want to focus on. Don't get down on yourself about it, just see it as a new opportunity to push yourself a little bit in those areas.

We all are a work in progress and balancing your life is going to be something that you are constantly working towards. And that's okay because when it comes to personal development, this wheel is a great place to start.

I am constantly working on areas of my life that I feel need to improve. I probably have hundreds of self-help, positive-thinking, how-to-make-life-great books. I'm usually picking up a new book to read in an area of my life where I feel the most lack at that time. Personal development—that is how we evolve as a person, that is how we continue to grow.

When you stop caring, stop pushing, stop growing, that is when we tend to get really dissatisfied with our lives. Then we start searching for unhealthy things in a quest to find some sort of joy again. It is imperative that we keep the important things in life in front of us at all times and when one of those areas get weak, we just work at getting it back on track.

Being healthy is all about balance. And it's about balancing a lot more than just your workout schedule and eating so-called "healthy" foods. That is just one facet of living a healthy life, feeling fulfilled, and having a sense of joy. I have spent so much of my life out of balance. Focused on things that I saw as extremely important in fulfilling some kind of happiness and joy in my life that truly was never going to be attainable by conquering this one specific area. As I said earlier, my quest for the perfect body was never going to be achieved! It was never going to be achieved because there is no such thing. All I can strive for is to have a healthy body—on the inside and out.

All I can do is work hard at loving myself, being happy with my decisions, and knowing when I decide to do something I do it because I love it not because I'm trying to make someone else love me. I am learning to take chances and push myself and to trust in God's perfect plan for my life.

I have to stop letting fear make decisions for me. I have to remember to continually search for that passion in my life that makes me excited to get up every morning. Without finding something that gets you excited to get out of bed every day, life can become so mundane and a very boring, sad place to live. God did not put us here on this earth to live mundane, boring, joyless, lives. We all must start finding the joy in every day.

We have to stop being so hard on ourselves and watching everyone else's lives. We have got to teach our children about passion at an early age so that they grow up knowing what it is like to exist in that realm.

We all must learn to find joy in the gloomy rainy days. We have to learn that the joy is in the journey not necessarily the destination.

We have to stop setting ourselves up for failure, thinking that there's something that we are missing in our lives because of what we see everybody else doing. Because we see everyone else's passion in life and what they're accomplishing and we feel less then because we are not doing what they are doing.

Find what makes you happy—find your passion—find what gets you excited to get out of bed every morning—then get out there and go for it. No matter what it is. No matter how irrelevant it may seem to others, if it is something that means something to you then do it. Live a life full of adventure and stop being so hard on yourselves, stop comparing yourself to others and practice living in a place of joy and gratitude. Remember:

Don't compare your life to someone else's highlight reel. You never know where their journey has taken them.

Take your own journey.

Keynote speaker at an American Diabetes Association Gala.

My prayer is that my own daughters will find their true passion in life.

Evening out at an event

Extended family selfie

Christmas Eve unfiltered.

Getting a nice family picture is always a challenge with this crew!

WE DID IT!

Acknowledgements

To all the amazing women who have had an influence on my life and helped me grow into the woman I am today, I say THANK YOU!

To all my future influencers, I look forward to meeting you!

About the Author

Lisa Moser's passion is to inspire people to live their best life and stop comparing themselves to others. As author, coach, and speaker, she has a love for educating and encouraging others to flourish in every aspect of a well-balanced, healthy lifestyle. Lisa is also a health and wellness educator, hairstylist, make-up artist, and owner of Positive Change 4U LLC. She and her husband, Don, are blessed with 4 amazing children.

Lisa started her journey and love for encouraging and motivating when she won the title of Miss Ohio USA and competed in the nationally televised Miss USA pageant. She spent her year traveling extensively, speaking to youth on positive self-image and being physically and mentally fit. In 1998, she returned to pageantry, won the title of Mrs. Ohio, and went on to win the national title of Mrs. International. During her reign as Mrs. International, she was the national spokesperson for the American Diabetes Association and worked with an international pharmaceutical company. She spent her year of service traveling with her children's book—*I Know Someone with Diabetes*—and educating people about diabetes.

She is still very active with raising awareness and funds for diabetes research. Lisa was also an educator and speaker for an international hair care company and an international health and wellness company. Presently, Lisa does motivational speaking throughout the United States to corporations, sports teams, health and wellness organizations, as well as at conferences, churches, and women's organizations and events. You can learn more about Lisa and her business, Positive Change 4U, at www.LisaMoser.com

I would love for you to connect with me and learn more about my services, events, and other programs.

www.LisaMoser.com
www.facebook.com/LisaMoserLive/
Instagram and Twitter @LisaMoserLive
www.linkedin.com/in/lisa-moser-b7019510/

Feel free to email me at:
lisa@LisaMoser.com

www.ingramcontent.com/pod-product-compliance
Lightning Source LLC
LaVergne TN
LVHW021048100526
838202LV00079B/4809